Praise for *The Art of Self-Leadership*

"The Art of Self-Leadership *is a powerful and comprehensive step-by-step guide for personal development. I highly recommend this book to anyone who wants to be deliberate about their leadership journey!*"

—Chris McChesney,
coauthor of
The 4 Disciplines of Execution

"The Art of Self-Leadership *is a powerful guide that encourages us to take responsibility for our growth and leadership. Heather Younger shows how true leadership starts from within, helping us build trust, belonging, and empowerment in our teams. With practical insights and real-life examples, Heather highlights how self-leadership fosters positive work cultures. Her approach emphasizes personal growth and the power of feedback, inspiring us to create environments where people feel valued and heard. This book is essential for anyone looking to lead with heart and purpose.*"

—Garry Ridge,
The Culture Coach; Chairman
Emeritus, WD-40 Company

"*All great leaders know the hardest person to lead is yourself. If you want a manual on how to do this well, this book is for you. In it you will find a model that helps guide you to reflect on the toughest challenges and address areas that may stop you from being the leader this world so greatly needs.*"

—David Ashcraft,
President and CEO,
Global Leadership Network

THE ART OF SELF-LEADERSHIP

THE ART OF
SELF-
LEADERSHIP

DISCOVER THE POWER WITHIN YOU
AND LEARN TO LEAD YOURSELF

HEATHER R. YOUNGER

WILEY

Published by John Wiley & Sons, Inc., Hoboken, New Jersey.
Published simultaneously in Canada.

For general information on our other products and services or for technical support, please contact our Customer Care Department within the United States at (800) 762-2974, outside the United States at (317) 572-3993 or fax (317) 572-4002.

Wiley also publishes its books in a variety of electronic formats. Some content that appears in print may not be available in electronic formats. For more information about Wiley products, visit our web site at www.wiley.com.

Library of Congress Cataloging-in-Publication Data is Available:

ISBN 9781394283378 (Cloth)
ISBN 9781394283392 (ePDF)
ISBN 9781394283385 (ePUB)

Cover Design: Wiley
Cover Image: © arteria.lab/Shutterstock
Author Photo: Courtesy of Rebecca Bonner

SKY10093704_121724

I dedicate this book to my life experience. Without the ups and downs of my life, I would have no idea how to lead myself well, nor could I write the words I wrote in this book.

I hope the ideas in this book assist you on your journey to self-actualize your brilliance and increase your impact in this world.

Contents

Preface

If you're reading this book, you're like me: I am on a constant journey of self-discovery, moving in and out of self-doubt and sprinkled with bits of self-confidence. This oscillation was even more distinct for me as I navigated work life. I would often find myself buried in others' expectations of me, my work, what I "should" be doing, and how I "should" be acting. Then I spent a fair amount of time waiting for others to give me "green lights" before I would move forward and then pause to wait for their external validation. This all felt defeating.

I have always had a way of being that makes people want to lean in to tell me things. At work, coworkers and team members would often come to me frustrated about what their managers did or failed to do. They seemed to be in a consistent state of confusion about what they could do to influence their journey at work, with their boss and their career progression. They often wanted to operate in more of a "take charge," assertive way, but lacked the confidence to express their unique perspectives or even show all that they could do without first waiting for permission. Their lack of personal direction and their lower self-regard often debilitated them and made them act in ways that minimized their true brilliance. The lack of manager support didn't help at all.

In my personal life, I often act as friend and counsel to those who want to know the best course of action from a relationship management perspective. Should I act this way or that way in xyz set of circumstances? How can I get this person or that person to understand that I want them to take me seriously, or that I do care about their opinion?

Throughout my career as a workplace culture and employee engagement consultant, I have facilitated numerous employee focus groups and culture teams. I have also read countless open-ended employee survey comments and coached many leaders. Through these experiences, I have heard many of the same frustrations and concerns.

After what seems like a lifetime of hearing many of these reservations and struggles, I feel compelled to dig deep to help people understand the gaps and opportunities that exist for them to lead themselves more than they ever thought possible.

Throughout the book, you'll notice that I will include some interview excerpts from my podcast, *Leadership with Heart*, polls from my social followers, and some telling stories from my own life and the life of others.

At the end of each chapter, I provide a summary section titled "Bright Ideas for Self-Leadership," to help you synthesize the most important points of that chapter and determine the next best actions to take. I also created a Self-Leadership Feedback Self-Assessment and an Accountability model I call *Success Circles*, to help you get and stay on track on your journey. I will explain more of that in the conclusion.

This book is designed for anyone seeking to enhance their self-leadership skills, regardless of their current position or title. Whether or not you hold a formal supervisory role, this guide is valuable for individuals aiming to develop their personal leadership abilities. Coaches will find this book beneficial for both personal growth and assisting their clients, while managers can leverage its insights for their own development. Professionals from any industry can use the precepts to help grow in self-leadership.

Those who read this book will instantly feel more powerful, become more aware of self-imposed limitations, and realize the many ways that they can learn to lead themselves that inspire others to want to be around them more. This new way of being will allow them to progress in their careers and lives without constantly feeling like they are in a holding pattern to someone else's whims.

The more we grow in self-leadership, the more magnetic we become, the more confident we feel about ourselves, and thus the more confidence others place in us. This opens the door for a personal and professional life that is more by design than by accident. This way of being gives us a life full of purpose that draws us closer to who we are meant to be. I don't know about you, but this is a compelling reason to pursue *The Art of Self-Leadership*!

Keep shining!

—Heather R. Younger, JD, CSP
Denver, Colorado, 2024

Introduction: Unveiling Your Golden Core

It takes a lot to follow the beat of someone else's drum. It takes even more to hear our own drums, tweak, and adjust them to our liking, and then follow the beats that we choose in the manner that suits us best.

The dictionary definition of leadership is "the action of leading a group of people or an organization." I disagree. I believe leadership is a personal quality, not a job description. Having a manager title does not necessarily equate to real leadership. Leadership to me is a way of being that makes people around us want to follow, engage, trust, and go over and above, not out of any requirement to do so, but out of a voluntary desire to do so. These are people at home, work, in our community, and in our friend circles. Intentionality and action are at its core.

> *I believe leadership is a personal quality, not a job description.*

Interestingly, there is no dictionary definition for self-leadership. According to an article on PositivePsychology .com, "the term 'self-leadership' first emerged from organizational management literature by Charles C. Manz (1983), who later defined it as a 'comprehensive self-influence perspective that concerns leading oneself toward performance of naturally motivating tasks as well as managing oneself to do work that must be done but is not naturally motivating' (Manz 1986)" (Neuhaus 2020). It was discussed mainly in the context of it being the necessary gateway to leading other people, much like I re-introduced it in my previous book, *The Art of Caring Leadership*.

In 2021, I wrote *The Art of Caring Leadership*, which provided a behavioral framework for leaders to use to demonstrate more care toward those who look to them for guidance in some way. In that book, I wrote a chapter about self-leadership. It was the first chapter and the longest by far, because, after all my research, I realized that it wasn't possible to demonstrate caring leadership without first leading oneself. I am proud of that body of work, but quite honestly I didn't go far enough with defining self-leadership and providing a strong framework for people to follow and really live out. I also regret not making it completely clear that anyone, no matter their title, can cultivate self-leadership. This is part of the reason why I decided to write an entire book on the topic.

This book is going to take a different path. I will introduce a self-leadership model that is grounded more in self-discovery and self-empowerment and not necessarily with the focus of leading others. For our purposes, self-leadership will be defined as the journey of growing inwardly to shine outwardly, spiraling upwards through self-awareness, and purposeful action.

> *Self-leadership is the journey of growing inwardly to shine outwardly, spiraling upwards through self-awareness, and purposeful action.*

An acronym that helps ground us in this definition is GROW:

Growth: Developing oneself from within
Resilience: Bouncing back and moving forward with grace
Outwardly: Extending one's influence and impact into the world
Wisdom: Leveraging insights and experiences for continuous improvement

Let me share a story that perfectly illustrates definition.

In the heart of Bangkok lies the Temple of the Golden Buddha, where a magnificent statue stands not only as a sacred effigy but also as a testament to the resilience and undiscovered treasure within us all. This statue, which weighs a staggering 5.5 tons and stands about 10 feet tall, is made of pure, solid gold and is valued at hundreds of millions of dollars. Yet the true value of this statue is not merely in its monetary worth but in the story it tells – a story that perfectly encapsulates the essence of self-leadership.

For centuries, the Golden Buddha was encased in a layer of stucco and colored glass, a disguise created by Thai monks to protect it from invading armies. The disguise was so convincing that everyone, including the invaders, overlooked it, seeing it as nothing more than an ordinary clay statue, albeit a large one. Not until 1955 was the true nature of the Buddha accidentally discovered, when the statue was dropped while being moved, revealing the brilliant gold underneath.

I learned of this story for the first time in January 2024 at a retreat meant to focus us on what was most important in the coming year and getting results based upon this renewed focus. The promise was that we would begin to receive blessings and even messages about what we say that we want before or after the retreat. While I remained hopeful, I was a little doubtful. The facilitator shared this story of the Golden Buddha in the context of self-actualization as a byproduct of our work during the retreat. We all hoped to discover some new, transformative insights and come out of it with renewed vigor. I was slightly intrigued when I heard this story, but what happened the next day is what shocked and amazed me.

I attended Mass on the morning of the second full day of the retreat at a local church not far from the retreat site. I sat there prayerful, listening and just taking in the beautiful surroundings. At the usual point in the liturgy, the deacon began to deliver his homily. To my delight and surprise, he shared the exact same story of the Golden Buddha. I chuckled under my breath. I had never heard this story in my life and now I had heard it two times in less than 24 hours? I saw this as one of the messages I needed to hear and as an extension of my retreat learning. The parallel that the deacon drew to this story was regarding a local school that he saw as "hidden" in their community in plain sight, but the school and its students needed to be revealed and nurtured, much like that Golden Buddha. They had so much to offer the world, but no one knew about it. As he described it, the community had placed so much clay over the school that no one could get to its core goodness. This deacon wanted to do his part to make sure those at Mass that day realized the school's brilliance.

This tale serves as a metaphor for the focus of this book and what needs to happen to us and inside us. Like the Golden Buddha, each of us is layered with a protective covering – made up of self-doubt, societal expectations, and fear of the unknown. These layers often prevent us from recognizing our true worth and the potential that gleams within. *The Art of Self-Leadership* is about peeling back these layers, chip by chip, helping to reveal the "golden" core within each of you and then using these insights to learn to lead yourself more effectively.

Much like the retreat facilitator and deacon were vessels for a powerful message of hope, empowerment, and personal awareness, let this book serve as a reminder of what is inside of you, act as a roadmap to reveal all of your brilliance, and help you achieve more and be more no matter your title or position.

As we embark on this journey together, let the Golden Buddha inspire you. Your external persona, shaped and colored by your experiences, triumphs, and tribulations, is but a protective layer. Beneath it lies your authentic self – resilient, valuable, and waiting to be rediscovered. Self-leadership is the hammer and chisel with which you will gently remove the covering to reveal your inner brilliance.

Through this book, you will learn to lead yourself with wisdom, courage, and compassion. You will uncover the strategies to nurture your intrinsic worth, much like the monks who carefully maintained the Buddha's disguise while knowing the treasure that lay underneath. Each chapter will guide you closer to that moment of revelation, to a place where you don't simply lead yourself but can also inspire leadership in others by the mere act of being your truest self.

I have divided this book into three parts that follow an Integrative Self-Leadership Development Model (see Figure I.1). This model serves as a unifying framework for the book, emphasizing the holistic development of your leadership qualities, starting from self-understanding and moving toward external expression and impact wrapped up with the bow of continuous improvement. I broke the book down into three parts as a definitive way for us to think about what is required for true self-leadership. My goal with this model is to take the vaguer concept of

FIGURE I.1 Integrated Self-Leadership Model™.

self-leadership and give you real steps to take to grow in this way of being. The following lists break down how this model integrates with the chapters to help you see the big picture.

- **Part I: Foundation of Self-Understanding**
  - Chapter 1, "Understanding Your Intrinsic Worth," explains that no matter what else I teach you, if you don't or can't understand who you are and your purpose on this planet, nothing else will matter.
  - Chapter 2, "Understanding Your Limitations," acknowledges the boundaries of your abilities as a starting point for your growth.
  - Chapter 3, "Understanding Fear," addresses your fears and barriers to your self-leadership.

- **Part II: Personal Growth and Sustainability**
  - Chapter 4, "Deciding Between Progress and Perfection," encourages you to focus on continual improvement rather than unattainable ideals.
  - Chapter 5, "Prioritizing Self-Care," ensures that self-maintenance is a priority for sustainable leadership, integrating self-grace and self-compassion amid challenges and mistakes.
  - Chapter 6, "The Three Stages of Empowerment," outlines a pathway for increasing your self-efficacy and autonomy.
  - Chapter 7, "Keying in on Your Strengths," shifts the focus to leveraging your personal strengths for leadership development.

- **Part III: Social Interaction and Influence**
  - Chapter 8, "Relationship-Building in Action," encourages your constructive engagement with others.
  - Chapter 9, "Leaning into Flexible Thinking," advocates for your flexibility and creativity in problem-solving.

- Chapter 10, "Expect Clear Expectations," stresses the importance of your self-advocacy.
- Chapter 11, "Feedback Is a Gift," frames feedback as a critical tool for your growth and improvement.
- Chapter 12, "Use Your Voice and Be Seen," encourages your assertiveness and visibility as mechanisms to expand your influence.

This model emphasizes a journey from internal self-awareness and self-compassion through personal development and mastery, to external application and influence. It underlines the importance of continuous learning, adaptability, and the effective integration of feedback. Each chapter of this book can be seen as a step in this journey, offering you a comprehensive guide to developing your self-leadership capacities in a structured, integrative manner. It will help connect your personal development to your external influence. My accountability system, found at the end of this book, will also help you stay on track on your journey.

So let us begin this journey of self-discovery, of chipping away the ordinary to reveal the extraordinary. In doing so, may you lead yourself to a life of purpose, fulfillment, and authentic self-expression.

I

Foundation
of Self-Understanding

At the core of my self-leadership model sits the most important thing we need to uncover if we want to show our brilliance: self-understanding. This is like playing the game Monopoly. You cannot pass Go and collect $200 dollars unless you have a true understanding of who you are and why you are on this planet. This is our starting point.

I chose "Understanding Your Intrinsic Worth" as the first chapter because it establishes the core value of self that underpins all of your further development. That chapter goes deep and will, most likely, drum up some emotions and memories that you didn't know were as critical in your formation. The remaining chapters in Part 1 help you understand the things that could and should be holding you back from choosing this path or that path in your journey.

Understanding Your Intrinsic Worth

Self-Awareness as the Bridge

A conversation about self-leadership and intrinsic worth is not possible without first discussing the importance of self-awareness. In social psychology, self-awareness can be traced back to the work of Shelley Duval and Robert Wicklund. They proposed that, at any given time, people can focus their attention on self or on the external environment. Focusing on *self* allows people to compare themselves to a standard of correctness and thus change their thoughts and behaviors in line with those standards ("Self-Awareness Theory" 2024). This is why self-awareness is necessary to have any self-control or in managing one's response to external stimuli.

When we think of self-leadership, we cannot lead ourselves if we aren't aware of how we are feeling, how we are responding, what we have affinities to and biases against, or even valid gauges on our achievements.

Recognizing Unique Qualities and Contributions

I want to dig deep here to challenge you to think about the dependence you might have on external validation and why this can jeopardize your ability to effectively lead yourself. I will delve into the ways you can uncover your unique value, which is critical in both personal and professional life. Together, we will explore potential roadblocks to true self-discovery, such as imposter syndrome, lack of confidence, negotiating based upon your own value, your ability to communicate your worth and boundaries, and burnout as the ultimate roadblocks to demonstrating strong self-leadership attributes.

This is an important chapter, because it will be difficult to continue this journey of self-discovery if we do not get to the bottom of many of these issues. As it is often said, "We need to get out of our own way." Said differently, "We are our own worst enemy." In the context of a self-leadership discussion, our ability to be our own solution versus the thing that stands in the way of our success is the only way through and to the life we want our for ourselves.

Our ability to be our own solution versus the thing that stands in the way of our success is the only way through and to the life we want for ourselves.

The Role of External Validation

I was tempted to get philosophical in this chapter because a focus on intrinsic worth (often referred to as "self-worth") has so many dimensions in that world. For our purposes, I want to keep this simple. Intrinsic worth is the value that we have by our very existence. Ideally, we should feel good because we are alive, we exist, and therefore we are good. That's it. No other proof needed. You are great and wonderful and worthy of all you want just by being.

Do you feel worthy just because you are alive?

If you're like me, you sometimes struggle with owning your intrinsic worth and feel like your life is a constant measure against others' ideas of what you should be. You seek validation or recognition from others, and whether or not you get it determines, in your mind, whether you do, in fact, feel good enough.

It should not be like this. We have got to stop holding on to that internal dialogue.

I have a confession: This might be my number one barrier to leading myself more effectively than I do now. I am an only child, and early in my life I received many nonverbal and verbal messages that I wasn't good enough or worthy. I was born into an interracial, interfaith family, and my maternal grandparents rejected different parts of me from the beginning. Growing up, I was excluded from many large family events, because I was who I was and because of what I looked like.

Later on, like most women (and on top of my already beat-up self-confidence), I received messages that I was too fat, or my hair was too straight or too curly, which also meant I wasn't good enough. Unfortunately, I believed those words and cues. For a long time, I did not feel good enough. Only in my 50s am I coming to terms with the fact that I am good, because I am.

In this book's introduction, I mentioned a retreat I attended where I first learned about the Golden Buddha. On the very last day of that retreat, I came to realize that I had an underlying belief that was holding me back: *I did not feel worthy of the things I said I wanted* and many others in the room felt the same way about themselves. It was just recently that I finally understood that I deserve to be more and have more of what I want. By not believing in myself, I was my own worst enemy.

Something that has helped me when my mind wanders into the self-sabotaging dialogue is this mantra (repeat it with me): "I am good, because I am."

I have read this message when reading the Bible or reading reflections, but it's not always easy to make it sink in. Once we get this truth to stick in our minds as true, we can begin to look at the pitfalls of seeking external validation to increase our worth.

The Pitfalls of External Validation

Yes, it's true. Many of us do all kinds of things to seek recognition or external validation of our worth. In recent years social media has only exacerbated this issue. Millions of people, including me and most of you, take to social platforms to get as many likes and hearts and comments and followers and shares as possible. The creators of these platforms understand our psyche better than we do. Since the majority of us doubt our self-worth, the creators of those platforms got filthy rich on their awareness that we deeply want external validation of who we are as a form of acceptance many of us never really felt we had. They bet we would get addicted to that validation. Their bets paid off and are still paying off. We are hooked!

Is the solution to get off social media? No, that wouldn't be realistic, although the people who voluntarily delete these apps and turn off the notifications are much more content with their lives than those of us who live in comparison mode for our use of these platforms (Southern 2023). Many have reported to me that they are less stressed, less self-critical, more energized by human interaction – the list of benefits goes on. Will I give it up anytime soon? Probably not. No matter, we need to be aware of the impact to our emotional well-being and how much the time we spend there negates any work we do to deeply understand the concept "I am good because I am."

At work, we have this same addiction. We are waiting for and seeking out validation from coworkers and our managers. It's like an unending search for the dopamine we experience every time we receive recognition. Unfortunately, that steady stream will come to an end. We need to find a way to ground

> *We need to find a way to ground ourselves in our own self-worth, learning to validate ourselves.*

ourselves in our own self-worth, learning to validate ourselves.

Overreliance on external validation can undermine self-leadership because, by definition, self-leadership includes growing inwardly to shine outwardly. That requires a knowledge and appreciation of what's already inside us. It will be hard or almost impossible to get there if all our worth is tied up in others' views of us. How can we ever measure up? What if we do not have the same value system? Will they ever see you the way you see you?

Self-Validation Practices

If external validation is the antithesis of self-leadership, then self-validation is the wind beneath your wings. In other words, self-validation is accepting your own internal experience, your thoughts, and your feelings (Hall 2014). Validating your thoughts and emotions will help you calm yourself and manage them more effectively. Validating yourself will help you accept and better understand yourself, which leads to a stronger identity and better skills at managing intense emotions. Self-validation helps you find wisdom (Hall 2014).

You will notice that this ties very closely to the self-awareness I mentioned earlier in this chapter, because we need to be aware of ourselves in profound ways, by taking the time to center on our thoughts and blocking out outside influences.

I see self-validation on three levels: our past thoughts, our past behaviors, and our present reality. All three of these are grounded in self-awareness and using mindfulness to center ourselves in these areas. When we think of our past, it might drum up thoughts of shame about something that happened to us, fear that the thing could happen again, and apprehension about our ability to conquer that thing in the future. We might doubt ourselves completely because of how we handled or failed to handle something before. We might even see that our past fully dictates our outcomes today.

Why do we judge ourselves so harshly, yet work harder to give others grace? A recent March 2024 LinkedIn poll conducted by Employee Fanatix asked, "What do you think contributes most to self-doubt and imposter syndrome when attempting to assert your voice in the workplace?" and 42% of respondents cited fear of making mistakes and past experiences of criticism. Unfortunately, many of us feel the same way. We have allowed external voices to overshadow our own. We have not worked on listening to our own voices and ignoring the others as we do so. What we need to do is to focus on recognizing the emotions we have regarding our past thoughts and behaviors, normalize or accept that those emotions are valid and justified, and then just lean into who we are wholeheartedly and without judgment.

In my earlier personal story, I felt a lot of rejection from my mother's side of the family, which made me doubt my own value, worth, and deservedness on so many levels. I was explicitly excluded from going to weddings, bar mitzvahs, funerals, and most family events. I remember wondering why I could not attend my own grandfather's funeral and why my dad wasn't allowed to attend many of these events. Without any direct explanation, I began to draw my own conclusions. That maybe I would stick out, that my family was ashamed of me, that I was never going to be enough to fit in. For much of my life, I allowed those external voices and judgments to be my truth.

After many years of feeling like this I had a realization: I needed to realize that I am on this planet for a reason and it was not to be the brunt of someone else's views of the world. I exist separate and apart from anything that any one person could think of me. No one else could grant me access to my life like I could. That realization turned my life around. I started to get to know myself, and with time I realized what my unique value was. We'll get more into that in Chapter 7.

Identifying Value Through Your Values

So how do you reveal your unique value if you are not quite sure what that is? Let's dive into how to discover your unique strengths and then make them known. When I was very young and saw Reverend Jesse Jackson on TV speaking to a large group of people, I remember being enthralled by how he captivated an audience through his words. I was intrigued and wondered if I could ever do that. I wanted to do that.

I was an outcast in my own family, and the only person who really pushed me to think outside of my current circumstances was my maternal grandmother. My relationship with her was a complicated one filled with confusion, exclusion, and a special kind of love. My maternal grandparents were white and Jewish and my paternal grandparents were Black and Christian. In today's world, this type of diversity is normal, but not in the 1960s and 1970s when my parents were dating and then married. My mom's parents had a hard time with this union, and then there I was, right in the middle of all the not-so-great emotions. I often felt like the black sheep of the family, being excluded from large family gatherings or public events, which made me feel unworthy. It also did not help that I was an only child.

One of the things my maternal grandmother pushed me to be was a lawyer. It was often hard to reconcile her strong belief that I should and *could* be a lawyer with the way my family treated me. I wanted to believe it, and at the same time a little part of me hoped that going to law school and achieving such a lofty accomplishment would finally make me "good enough" in my grandparents' eyes and end the exclusion.

I thought maybe if I became a lawyer, I would finally get their approval and be accepted as part of the family. Maybe, as a lawyer, I could attend family gatherings.

I did end up going to law school, graduating a semester earlier than my class and passing the bar the first time, but something in me knew this accomplishment was not for the right reasons. In law school, I discovered I had a real knack for presenting to people in an authentic way. It was affirmed by different groups on different occasions. Interestingly, I only practiced law for a few years and then quit the practice of law after acknowledging it was not a unique strength or talent I possessed or even wanted.

Honestly, besides presenting to people and marketing the law firm, I hated the practice of law. There was so much law library research and writing legal briefs. I thought to myself, "Is this what my life will be like?" I was miserable. I left the practice of law to go work as a sales consultant for Mary Kay cosmetics. I don't know how many people can say, "I quit the practice of law to sell Mary Kay cosmetics."

Not that there's anything wrong with selling Mary Kay cosmetics, but I had worked toward this "dream" of becoming a lawyer for so long that leaving it brought back a lot of those "I'm not good enough" feelings again.

Truthfully, I discovered a lot about my true talents while working for Mary Kay. I discovered that I was a pretty good salesperson, I really enjoyed helping others grow and take the time to develop themselves, and I was persuasive. I had a moderate amount of success, earning a car and becoming a sales director quickly. Having said that, I also discovered that I was using some of my talents more for my benefit and not as much for others. Over time, I did not like what I saw in myself and the person I was turning into. I decided it was time to move on to hone in on the desire and strength of growing and leading people. That's when my corporate career began, which eventually led me to where I am today.

Your brilliance is also shown by uncovering and living your core values and then knowing how they contribute to your sense of worth. Think about it. We grow in our sense of self when we know our values, embody them daily, and then positively impact others by demonstrating them consistently. When I think of value embodiment, I think of Nelson Mandela, former president of South Africa and Nobel Peace Prize winner. Mandela dedicated his life to fighting apartheid in South Africa and promoting values of equality, justice, and reconciliation. He spent 27 years in prison for his anti-apartheid activities, emerging as a symbol of resilience and commitment to his cause. Upon his release, Mandela continued his fight, eventually becoming South Africa's first Black president. His presidency and the rest of his life were marked by efforts to dismantle the legacy of apartheid through building a racially inclusive new South Africa, emphasizing forgiveness and reconciliation. His unwavering commitment to these values, even after enduring tremendous personal hardship, makes him a profound example of self-leadership and moral integrity (Nelson Mandela Foundation n.d.).

What do you value most? Do you know what your core values are? Here is a list of the most common core values. Do any of these resonate? Choose the top five from this list and reflect on how well you demonstrate these consistently:

- Integrity: Acting with honesty, transparency, and ethical behavior in all situations

- Respect: Treating others with kindness, empathy, and consideration, regardless of differences
- Responsibility: Taking ownership of one's actions, decisions, and commitments
- Compassion: Showing empathy, care, and concern for the well-being of others
- Authenticity: Being true to oneself and expressing genuine thoughts, feelings, and intentions
- Courage: Facing challenges, adversity, and fear with bravery and determination
- Gratitude: Recognizing and appreciating the blessings and opportunities in life
- Perseverance: Persisting in the pursuit of goals and overcoming obstacles with resilience
- Empathy: Understanding and sharing the feelings and experiences of others
- Collaboration: Working cooperatively and respectfully with others to achieve common goals
- Growth: Continuously seeking learning, development, and self-improvement
- Fairness: Upholding principles of justice, equality, and fairness in interactions and decisions
- Generosity: Sharing resources, time, and support with others without expecting anything in return
- Creativity: Embracing innovation, imagination, and originality in thinking and problem-solving
- Balance: Striving for harmony and equilibrium in all aspects of life, including work, relationships, and well-being

I invite you to also think about and document the times in your life you are most proud of and are most memorable. What values were in full display during those times and how did those times shape you?

_____

_____

Times in my life that were the most memorable:

_____

_____

Finally, jot down who the role models are in your life. Which values do they embody the most?

Role Model One: _____

Role Model Two: _____

Role Model Three: _____

The values you value are either already in you or have the potential to be there. You aren't that far from pinpointing them. Once you do, you will begin to reveal the power within you.

Next, let's look at the role of self-confidence in understanding your own worth.

The Role of Self-Confidence

Self-confidence is a feeling of trust in our own abilities.

Self-confidence is not an overall evaluation of yourself, but a feeling of confidence and competence in more specific areas. For example, you could have a high amount of self-worth but low self-confidence when it comes to extreme sports, certain subjects in school, or your ability to speak a new language (Ackerman and Nash 2018).

It's not necessary to have a high sense of self-confidence in every area of your life; there are naturally some things that you will simply not be very good at, and other areas in which you will excel. The important thing is to have self-confidence in the activities in your life that matter to you and a high sense of self-worth overall.

The important thing is to have self-confidence in the activities in your life that matter to you and a high sense of self-worth overall.

In the context of self-leadership, which has at its foundation "growing inwardly to shine outwardly," our acquisition and retention of strong self-confidence are crucial in our journey to developing the ability to lead ourselves well.

Let's broach the subject of the elephant in the room in many of our lives as it relates to what gets in the way of our having confidence: imposter syndrome. "People who struggle with imposter syndrome believe that they are undeserving of their achievements and the high esteem in which they are, in fact, generally held. They feel that they aren't as competent or intelligent as others might think – and that soon enough, people will discover the truth about them" (*Psychology Today* n.d.).

To dig deeper on this I conducted a LinkedIn poll that got more than 100 responses. When asked, "How often have you experienced imposter syndrome in your daily life?" only 11% answered "Never," but 47% reported "Sometimes," and 38% reported "Pretty Often." This is revealing. Feeling like an imposter is not something that burdens just the few, but the many.

I have a confession to make. I have felt like an imposter many times in my life, with those feelings of doubt or lack of worthiness, especially when I have achieved something lofty, or was in the process of trying to achieve it. I love how Dr. Melissa Hughes talks about imposter syndrome as being our "inner critic." Dr. Hughes explains imposter syndrome in the context of brain science:

The brain's primary job is to keep us alive. So it's always scanning for danger. . . .The worst thing about the amygdala is that it can literally hijack the thinking brain, the last to develop. . . .The thinking brain doesn't fully develop until closer to the age of 25. . . .Our neuro priorities are first to survive, second, to feel and third, to think. The Zeigarnik effect is your inner critic filibustering a million reasons why you're not good enough, smart enough, whatever enough.

—*Hughes 2017*

These insights from Dr. Hughes provide clarity regarding how our brain allows imposter syndrome to take hold. If our focus is first to survive, then when we feel even the smallest amount of fear or apprehension around our ability to achieve or even what might happen if we succeed in anything, that inner critic often puts us in survival mode.

There is a difference between having a strong self-worth and having strong self-confidence in that self-worth is more about you valuing yourself and feeling that you are a good person who deserves to be treated with respect. So when we evaluate our own self-confidence, we might ask, "Do I not have the skills to do it right now? What steps do I need to take to be able to accomplish this? Is this even something I'm good at?" On the other hand, when we doubt our self-worth, we might think, "Do I deserve to achieve this or be awarded this thing or that thing?"

Do you see the difference? One is a way we see ourselves at the core and is more limited thinking, and the other is more about being ready at a moment in time to accomplish a specific thing or task. Thus it's almost impossible to have strong self-confidence if we are in a constant state of doubting our worth. Then we can build self-confidence through several approaches.

It's almost impossible to have strong self-confidence if we are in a constant state of doubting our worth.

So how do we overcome imposter syndrome?

Overcoming imposter syndrome involves changing a person's mindset about their own abilities. Imposters feel like they don't belong, so acknowledging their expertise and accomplishments is key, as is reminding themselves that they earned their place in their academic or professional environment.

People should stay focused on measuring their own achievements, instead of comparing themselves to others. Similar to perfectionists, people with impostorism often put a lot of pressure on themselves to complete every task flawlessly; they fear that any mistake will reveal to others that they aren't good or smart enough for the job.

—Psychology Today n.d.

I find the parallel from this quote about the person who feels like they are an imposter and the one who is a perfectionist interesting. Both do not feel good enough and fear doing anything that will reveal their imperfection. While I will discuss perfectionism in more detail in Chapter 4, you can see how this type of thinking can ruin your sense of worth and debilitate your ability to pull yourself up and lead others well. Our biggest task? Compare ourselves to ourselves and not to others.

Once we overcome imposter syndrome and increase our sense of self-worth, we can build self-confidence by reflecting on multiple strategies.

Case Study

Gina, a Recreation Director:

I spent many years feeling imposter syndrome, because I had worked my way up in a career where everyone had a degree. Unfortunately, I believe I was self-sabotaging by not always giving my all because I did not feel good enough. I eventually lost my job of 17 years. I would read a lot about the numerous successful people that started world class businesses without degrees. That helped a little. I have reinvented myself. Went back to school to get a degree in finance and although the degree has helped me overcome the feeling a little, I've come to the realization that no one really knows or feels that they know what they are doing. We all feel the same way for the most part.

One more thing, the turning point for me. I have been working with a coach for almost two years. When I first started with her, I remember talking about imposter syndrome and actually feeling like I was labeling something that was really something else. It turns out for me, it was really more about fear. Being afraid to put myself out there and in many ways being fearful of my own success and power. Now I am in place of exploration. Knowing that I belong and my contributions matter, along with what everyone else has to offer. I was able to reframe this to where I am not afraid of failure. Knowing everyone fails and the power of learning from my failures ignites my creativity and drive. Some great advice I received was that if someone does not like what you're selling, move on.

To the other part. My parents did not have degrees. I grew up with very little direction or discipline, something I tell my parents today. We have a great relationship today. When I was growing up, I had way too much freedom to do whatever I wanted. Luckily, I did not get into too much trouble. I had to learn to plan, focus, and implement – something I still struggle with today (personal communication, May 6, 2024).

What I appreciate most from Gina's story is all of the proactive things she did to help herself thrive. She did not wait for external validation; she fought to make sure she no

(*continued*)

(*continued*)

longer saw herself as an imposter, but as a self-worthy and self-confident individual. She did not make herself a victim because of her parent's lack of formal education or even their lack of providing her direction. Did you also notice how she researched her own growth strategies? She is a great example of owning her own journey and learning to lead herself.

Strategies for Building Self-Confidence

Pursue a Degree or Certification

Much like Gina's case study above, sometimes pinpointing and then completing a new degree program can help to increase your confidence, because you feel more prepared to conquer new career paths. Your vision of your abilities and future becomes clearer too.

Commit to Lifelong Learning

Admittedly, I have not always been the greatest at constantly learning new topics or venturing out, but I am growing in this focus. I can think of a few amazing people who do this well. Both commit to reading up to one hundred books per year, watching educational shows, and enrolling in programs outside their normal areas of expertise. I learn a lot from them. They also inspire me to do the same. Does anyone inspire you, or are you serving as the inspiration for others?

Prepare for Success

You will read more about this in later chapters, but it is worth pointing out that the more we prepare for success, the more confidence we have. When I take time to double down on preparation before stepping on the stage to speak, the more confident I feel, and the looser I feel when I'm on stage. When I do not prepare enough, I focus more on myself and my fears than on serving the audience. Do you have a consistent practice of preparation?

Do Not Compare Yourself

I used to have a philosophy, which I would repeat to my kids often, that went like this: "Do not compare yourself to the worst, but only the best." The problem with this statement is that comparison is the recipe for a strong lack of self-worth and self-confidence. Also, I could not bring myself to feel happy for or good about the success of "the best." Finally, comparing your current state to what you perceive to be someone else's "best" is like comparing frogs to potato chips. There is no obvious comparison. Once I finally understood that, I could begin to feel good about what others were achieving in the world without it feeling like it diminished what I was contributing. That change in mindset was the most liberating thing I did for myself and the thing that allows me to lead myself more effectively than I ever have.

Accept the Good News

This one is hard for many of us. Of course, we can grow in confidence when someone sincerely compliments our work or we get recognition or awards for it. But if we do not believe them, because of our feeling of a general lack of self-worth, it won't matter anyway. Here's what I want you to know: as someone who wants to grow in self-leadership, you need to lean in to believe the good stuff just as much as you believe the not-so-great stuff. You are the creator of your own self-confidence. You cannot rely solely on others to get it. Stamp in your mind that the good stuff is yours to take too. When someone compliments you, just repeat in your head, "They are damn right I did a great job on that!" or "Hot damn, I am good!" or "My efforts, focus, and skills help me rock this!" Finally, adopt this thinking: "I take the good more than I take the bad." This just means that you place more weight on the good or constructive news than you do on the bad news. You are the one who protects your confidence. Remember, inward shine to outward brilliance!

Adopt an Abundance Mindset

One of things that can quickly shake our self-confidence is when we think there is only so much success to go around. Perhaps we often think of opportunities that come our way as "once in a lifetime," or we might naturally think that when someone else wins, we lose. This is not thinking in abundance. We need to adopt an abundance mindset and realize that just because that person or friend has achieved something wonderful, there is still plenty of wonderful left for us to seize as well.

> *When someone else has achieved something wonderful, we need to realize there is still plenty of wonderful left for us.*

I've fallen victim to this way of thinking before. In my profession as a speaker, I am often considered for speaking engagements right alongside some of my closest friends. Sometimes I'm selected and sometimes they're selected. That's just how it is and will always be. But I used to feel bad when I saw other speakers have a lot of success. It would prompt in me this feeling of "lack" or "scarcity" that shook my confidence in myself, my abilities, and what I stood for. Then I decided to change my thinking and see their success as wonderful. I no longer looked at it in the "me-versus-them," or "I am competing with them," or "They are better than I am" way. To the contrary, I began to realize that there is more than enough out there for us all. That we are meant to serve different clients at different times, for different reasons. This was a refreshing perspective, and it allowed me to finally take off the weights that were dragging down my confidence. I could be my best me and they could simultaneously be the best them. Adopt this mindset and it will truly set you free to find your self-confidence again.

Do a Skills Assessment

Understanding what we are amazing at and what we suck at are critical to building self-confidence. The key is to understand our strong foundational skills and then live most of our time there. I am not saying do not build new skills. I am saying hang out with your most obvious skills so that the shimmer in you remains most apparent to those around you.

Understanding what we are amazing at and what we suck at are critical to building self-confidence.

Think about it: When we take on something new, we are growing and learning, and sometimes we place clay over ourselves because we are not yet confident to show others. Of course, we have no issue removing the clay in areas we know are strongest. Revealing those requires less vulnerability. Have you done a skills assessment lately? I do think the StrengthsFinder I refer to at the end of the chapter can help, but just Google "free skills assessment" and you can take a number of assessments to help you understand your most natural skills. Then lean into those to stay in your highest confidence zone. Remember, you cannot lead another human soul until you lead yourself well first. Maintaining strong self-confidence is a part of that. Who wants to follow someone who is not even confident in their own whisper, let alone their own abilities?

To really grow in self-confidence, you have to make a fundamental shift in your thinking from "things need to be perfect all the time" to "progress over perfection" is best. I want to dive deeper into this concept in the next chapter.

Bright Ideas for Self-Leadership

Daily Self-Validation Practice

- Each morning or evening, spend 5–10 minutes journaling about your thoughts and feelings. Acknowledge and validate your emotions without judgment. Use the mantra "I am good, because I am" to reinforce your intrinsic worth. Reflect on moments when you felt proud or accomplished, and recognize the internal qualities that contributed to those experiences.

Identify and Live Your Core Values

- Choose your top five core values from the provided list in the earlier section "Identifying Value Through Your Values" (e.g. integrity, empathy, courage). For each value, write down one specific action you can take this week to demonstrate that value in your daily life. For instance, if "empathy" is a core value, plan to actively listen to a friend or colleague without interrupting. Reflect at the end of the week on how living these values impacted your sense of self-worth.

———————————————————
———————————————————
———————————————————
———————————————————
———————————————————

Self-Confidence Building Exercise

- Identify an area where you feel a lack of self-confidence. Set a small, achievable goal in this area for the week. For example, if public speaking is a challenge, commit to speaking up in one meeting or practicing a short presentation at home. After completing the goal, reflect on the experience, focusing on what you did well and what you learned. Repeat this exercise regularly to build incremental confidence.

Reduce Dependence on External Validation

- Conduct a one-week experiment where you limit your use of social media or seek feedback less frequently at work. Instead, focus on self-reflection and self-acknowledgment. Each day, write down three things you appreciate about yourself or your work, independent of others' opinions. Notice any changes in your mood and self-perception over the week.

Use Assessments

- Participate in assessments like the Myers-Briggs Type Indicator (MBTI), DiSC Profile, or StrengthsFinder. These assessments identify your personality traits, communication styles, strengths, and areas for development. The results offer valuable self-awareness by highlighting your natural inclinations and preferred ways of operating. Review the assessment outcomes and reflect on how these insights align with your experiences and observations. Use this self-awareness to leverage your strengths in various aspects of your life, including personal relationships, career choices, and skill development.

As we continue on our journey to self-understanding, we must consider our own limitations, both those self-imposed and those external to us.

2

Understanding Your Limitations

To deal with our limits, we must know what they are. When I speak about limits, I am referring more to your own self-imposed limits than to external constraints. Both are critical to your long-term success, but the first must be clear from the start, because if you are the biggest barrier to your own growth, advancement, and development, the work rests with you alone.

Self-imposed limits are those barriers we put up in our own way that stop us from achieving things we set out to do. When we underestimate our worth or value but maybe value others, we get in our own way. This could look like us choosing not to apply for a position at work because we think others applying have a better chance and better skills. We never even give ourselves the chance to compete.

External constraints – constraints imposed by others – are the many ways that our friends, family, or coworkers assume we can't do something, or choose to limit our potential, growth, and advancement based upon their perceptions, biases, and insecurities. We have much less control over the external side and 100% control over the internal side.

When we understand our limits to both personal and professional growth, it releases the pressure to be and do things that we are not and will never be. When we are confused about our limits, we venture into places that don't serve us or others to our highest potential. Think about it: if you are someone who values being around family often, but then you take on a role that requires you to be away from your family often, you will compromise your value structure and your happiness. Or perhaps you value close relationships with customers and meeting with them in person, but then you go to work for a company that you know does not allow for in-person meetings.

Understanding your limitations provides the type of clarity you need to make better decisions that benefit you and your personal and professional journey. You might be wondering, "Heather, this makes sense, but how do I identify my limits?" Let's go a little deeper on this topic.

Identifying Your Limits

In Chapter 1, I discussed how self-awareness is important for understanding our own intrinsic worth. Self-awareness is also important in recognizing your emotional, mental, and physical limits. If you find even walking around your neighborhood unpleasant, don't start planning a Mount Everest expedition. You have to consider your physical abilities and choose activities accordingly. As in the example above with your core value of spending time with family, for your own emotional and mental well-being, you wouldn't want to take a job a thousand miles away from your family.

Personally, I know all too well what it feels like to make decisions that are in direct contradiction to my limits. I mentioned earlier that I focused like a crazy person to go to law school and be a "lawyah" (how my Bronx-born grandma pronounced lawyer) like my grandmother wanted for me. I never really did any job shadowing of lawyers and law firms. I never got any internships to try that job beforehand, partly because I didn't know I should do that, and partly because I didn't have ready access.

Back then, high schools and colleges did not promote skills-based or personality assessments to identify good job matches. So I sort of went blindly into the profession. While I really enjoyed law school, I never really thought about why I enjoyed it. Then, when I was out in the real world working in a firm, I quickly realized I disliked the real-life practice of law, with the exception of marketing legal services and interacting with clients. With every hour I spent in law libraries or writing legal briefs, I was miserable. I was a withering vine waiting to be cultivated. I failed to recognize my deep desire to be relational with people, not with textbooks and libraries. My deep unhappiness showed in my work product and my general lack of focus on details, which is sort of critical as a lawyer. Once my limits became painfully apparent, I chose to switch my career altogether. If I had remained in that role or in that profession, I would have been living my life for someone else in perpetuity.

In the professional context, I am not sure I had the baseline skills to do that job. I struggled with how to integrate the research and the proper methods of legal writing. I tend toward wordy, flowery writing, but legal writing was more prescriptive and formulaic.

Another thing to consider is whether time permits us to achieve a task or project. Are you limited in your desire to achieve your work projects in the two weeks you want versus the five days you actually have? I remember discussing this with an audience member during one of my keynotes. She said that she always wants to take more time to reflect on and then prepare her thoughts and work response to people on the other end who want her opinion and work product very quickly. She admitted that she knew that two weeks was too long, but struggled with getting things done in the short period of time others wanted, given her need to evaluate things longer. I advised her to offer a compromise so that both would feel comfortable about achieving the end goal and in the most reasonable period of time.

While there might be environmental limits and boundaries affecting your ability to strive and thrive at work, in the context of self-leadership, it is important to focus more on your own self-imposed limits. You have a much better chance of quashing the ones that don't serve you and leaning in to the ones that do if you start your focus here.

Use the circle diagram shown in Figure 2.1 to help you define your limits and aid you in your decision-making.

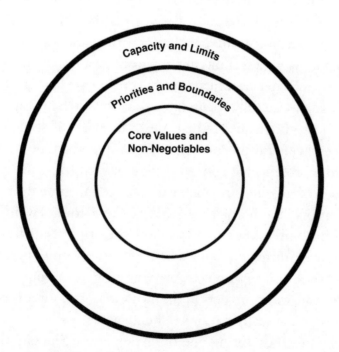

FIGURE 2.1 Limitations breakdown diagram.

This method involves drawing three concentric circles on a piece of paper or a whiteboard, each representing different aspects of your life:

1. Inner Circle – Core Values and Non-Negotiables: In the innermost circle, write down your core values, beliefs, and non-negotiables. These are the principles that you hold most dear and are unwilling to compromise on. They represent the foundation of who you are and what you stand for.

2. Middle Circle – Priorities and Boundaries: In the middle circle, list your priorities and boundaries. These are the things that are important to you and deserve your time, attention, and energy. They may include your family, health, career goals, personal development, and relationships. Setting clear boundaries around these priorities helps you maintain balance and prevent burnout.

3. Outer Circle – Capacity and Limits: In the outer circle, identify your capacity and limits. This includes your physical, emotional, mental, and time constraints. Be honest with yourself about what you can realistically handle and where you need to set boundaries to avoid overcommitting or spreading yourself too thin.

Once you have completed the circle diagram, take a step back and review your circles. Reflect on what you wrote down and consider how they influence each other. This visual representation can help you gain clarity on your personal and professional limits and guide you in making decisions that honor your values, priorities, and capacity.

The Role of Limits in the Workplace

This idea of understanding our own limits actually serves to protect you. Not placing limits in your life can take a toll on your health, especially at work. If you don't recognize your own limits emotionally, mentally, or physically, you'll probably experience burnout or stress or even overcommit to projects. That overall lack of self-awareness can hurt our chances of being all we can be for ourselves, our families, and at work. Have you ever overcommitted at work and then, too late to back out, you found yourself completely overwhelmed? That's what happens when you either don't understand your own limits or don't know how to communicate them.

If you don't get comfortable with your own self-imposed limitations, someone else will happily step in to limit your potential.

In our society where the motto is "The only limits you have are those that are in your mind," it can be really confusing and make us overextend ourselves to the point of burnout and a lack of real focus. Admitting that you have limits – and more importantly, choosing those limits – can be hard, but it is necessary if you are going to focus on what you are good at and shine brighter. If you don't get comfortable with your own self-imposed limitations, someone else will always be "the boss of you." Someone else will happily step in to limit your potential.

Personally, I know all too well the negative impacts of not placing limits on myself. About 15 years ago, I was working for a company and a boss that demanded a lot of me. I rarely felt supported by her, and it mostly felt like she would go out of her way to point out where I made mistakes. I felt like I was under a microscope. Things were getting tense at home too, and I was finding it hard to cope. I ignored the stress and just kept marching along. One day, while I was sitting in my office, I felt my face, eyelids, eyeballs, and one side of my arm go numb. I started to freak out and thought I was having a stroke. I anxiously stood up and walked to a team member's office and said, "I think I'm having a stroke. Can you take me to the ER?" She immediately jumped into action, grabbed her keys, and we headed out the door. At the ER, they conducted an EKG and other scans, which were all clear. They explained to me that I wasn't having a stroke, but a severe panic attack. They prescribed a few valium to get me to settle down.

I was so shocked that stress could turn into such physical symptoms. Following that episode, I started to see a therapist and learn how to use sunshine and deep-breathing to help calm myself. I am now much better at being self-aware of my own emotional limits.

Challenging and Expanding Limits

I remember being told either explicitly or implicitly to "stay in my lane" by people within and outside of my work. I have to be honest – I hate that idea! In my own mind, I choose my own lane *or lanes* and *when I move in and out of them.* Just because we identify our limits today doesn't mean those same limits exist a month or a year later. You need to continually evaluate your limits using the circle diagram from Figure 2.1 and also understand that it is wholly up to you how and when you challenge or expand those limits.

Just because we identify our limits today doesn't mean those same limits exist a month or a year later.

Limits don't minimize your ability to change your mind or your direction at some point. In fact, I think healthy stretching outside of your self-imposed limits is a good thing. There is a difference between constructive stretching and destructive overstepping. Understanding this difference and how it comes to life inside of you will ensure your success in your personal and professional life. On the destructive overstepping front, those around you will either directly or indirectly let you know you have shown a lack of respect or that you are stepping on their toes and outside of your job responsibilities. If you get this message, just review Figure 2.1 and decide whether you need to change any of the elements in the circles to align with your current role or the role you desire to be in.

It is often said that fear holds us back from doing what we dream of so we place false limits on ourselves that stop us from leading ourselves in powerful ways. Let's look next at whether fear is holding you back from true self-leadership.

Bright Ideas for Self-Leadership

Identify Self-Imposed Limits

- Reflect on a recent situation where you held back due to self-doubt (e.g. not applying for a job). Write down the thoughts and beliefs that stopped you. Challenge these beliefs by listing evidence or past experiences that prove you are capable. Make a plan to confront and overcome one of these self-imposed limits in the coming week.

Set Realistic Goals Based on Your Limits

- Choose one professional and one personal goal for the week that respects your identified limits. Ensure these goals are specific, measurable, achievable, relevant, and time-bound (SMART). For example, if you recognize that you need more time for personal reflection, set aside 30 minutes each day for this purpose. Evaluate at the end of the week how well you adhered to these goals and what adjustments you might need to make.

Practice Boundary Setting

- Think of a current responsibility or task that feels over-whelming or misaligned with your capacity. Plan a con-versation with a colleague, supervisor, or family member to renegotiate or set new boundaries around this task. Use clear and assertive communication to express your needs and limits, aiming for a mutually beneficial compromise. Reflect on the outcome of this conversation and its impact on your stress levels and productivity.

Our fears run deep. The choice we make to keep them with us or leave them behind directly impacts our ability to lead our-selves and others.

3

Understanding Fear

When thinking about self-leadership and the things that could hold us back from being a magnetic leader, with or without a formal manager title, we must understand and name our fears if we are to conquer them. Hiding from them only makes things worse and reduces the influence we have on those around us.

> *We must understand and name our fears if we are to conquer them.*

I think we all know what a fear is, but did you know that there are rational and irrational fears? A rational fear might mean that you are afraid when you run into a real-life lion. An irrational fear or phobia might be that you are paralyzed every time you see a spider. It's an irrational fear because there is a very low likelihood that a spider will do irreparable harm. It's important to know how to categorize the fears we have and also where they originated. Some fears are learned based upon our environment and others are based upon our personal experiences.

I grew up with drug addiction in my home. As an only child, that was often hard to decipher and manage. I had read that addiction can be passed down to children. So I often feared whether I would also become an addict in some way. From this very rational fear grounded in research, I developed a real, and sometimes irrational, fear around taking any form of medication, especially those that are known to be addictive in nature.

How did this phobia show up? I refused to take any pain medications during childbirth, because I was afraid it might taint my memory of the experiences. Instead, I chose to hire a doula to help me reduce pain in more natural ways. When I go to doctors and they want me to take medication, I rarely comply unless I really have a lot of pain. Most recently, my health coach wanted me to start on drops to curb appetite while also working to release weight and establish healthy eating patterns. I experienced so much anxiety around taking the drops that we decided to work together in a different way that would not require me to take the drops. I go out of my way not to take prescription drugs or pain medications, because I have that deep-seated fear that I might become addicted. Of course the media's reporting of opioid overdoses in cars and in bus stations by everyday people does not help. These fears have not stopped me from doing things that are important to me or my family, or achieving goals in my life. So I will most likely keep them where they are, but I know I will need to face them with the help of a therapist someday.

What other fear-based behaviors might we adopt depending on the circumstances? These behaviors can be the difference between us living our best and healthiest lives and us living on the edge and giving up so much of the personal power we possess to lead ourselves well and influence others.

Fear-Based Behaviors

Often, the things we fear can impact our decision-making, our ability to innovate, and even the morale of those around us. Below is a list of some fear-based behaviors that can thwart your effectiveness and your ability to show up and be seen as someone who leads themselves well:

> *The things we fear can impact our decision-making, our ability to innovate, and even the morale of those around us.*

- Procrastination: Sometimes, fear of failure can lead some individuals to procrastinate as a way to avoid facing potential disappointment or inadequacy. This delay can impede your progress and limit the achievement of your goals. I have been there and done that. I had some moments of procrastination even writing this book, wondering, "Will they think this is nonoriginal content?" or "Will anyone want to buy this?" Then I gently and figuratively slapped myself to keep going.

- Overplanning: For some, fear of uncertainty can lead to excessive planning. You might spend too much time on planning and preparation as a way to control every possible outcome, which can prevent you from actually taking the necessary actions to succeed.

- Risk aversion: Often, fear of taking risks can result in missed opportunities. This might manifest in someone staying in a comfortable but unfulfilling job, avoiding investments, or not pursuing innovative ideas. I remember staying in a few jobs a little longer than I needed to, because I was afraid of what I would do next. In my last job before starting my own business, I held on for about six months longer than I needed to while also working my side hustle almost full time too. It was a stressful time and one that highlighted my risk aversion for sure.

- Perfectionism: We will talk about this in detail in Chapter 4, but this fear-based behavior is driven by a fear of criticism or not being good enough. It can cause individuals to spend too much time perfecting details instead of moving forward with projects or decisions.

- Avoidance of feedback: Fear of negative feedback might cause some people to avoid situations where they could receive constructive criticism. This behavior can hinder your personal and professional growth. I will dive into the benefits of giving and receiving feedback in Chapter 11. Just know that all feedback is a gift.

- Social withdrawal: Often, fear of rejection or judgment might lead someone to withdraw from social or professional interactions, limiting their network and opportunities for collaboration or advancement. While sometimes this stems from social anxiety, which is more of a mental health challenge, many people simply limit their potential to develop into better self-leaders because of this behavior.

- Decision paralysis: When someone is fearful of making the wrong decision, it can lead to decision paralysis, where the person is unable to make a choice at all. This can severely limit their ability to progress in the path of their choice. I have definitely been here before. I usually seek out a friend who can help me see a way forward, which knocks me out of the stuck place and into productive action.

Do you recognize any of these behaviors? Are some of these more familiar than others? Fear is a natural part of being human. You will not be able to completely overcome every fear. In fact, a good dose of fear can be good for our health and life inside and outside of work.

The Nature of Fear in the Workplace

As we go back to ground ourselves in the inward-outward definition of self-leadership, let us look at the real nature of fear at work and how it impacts us and those around us.

There are various sources of fear at work and many can significantly impact your performance and well-being. Some common origins of fear in the workplace include:

- Job security: Fear of job loss is one of the most common fears among employees, especially in industries prone to layoffs or during economic downturns. I remember how this fear took hold in me when I was working for a company that was going through a merger. I could feel in my bones that my job was at risk. Unfortunately, my intuition was accurate.

- Performance anxiety: This makes people concerned about not meeting expectations or not being competent enough can create considerable anxiety. This is often exacerbated by high-pressure environments and demanding performance targets.

- Change and uncertainty: The fear of the unknown, such as changes in leadership, company direction, or job role, can lead to stress and anxiety. Humans generally prefer stability, and uncertainty can be unsettling. I think we are living in a world of constant change, which might mean many of us are walking around in constant fear of what we do not know. I know this is where I was through that big merger I mentioned above.

- Conflict: When looking at workplace fears, interpersonal issues, such as conflict with colleagues or managers, can lead to a fear of confrontation or retaliation. This can also include fear of discrimination, harassment, or even psychological safety.

- Overwork and burnout: Fear of burnout or being overwhelmed by workloads can lead to stress, especially in highly competitive environments where long hours are the norm. This might also make some lean into the procrastination that I mentioned above.

When organizational leaders consider the triggers for fear, they can work to put processes in place to address each. For the purpose of this book, I want you to understand how fear might affect your psyche and even show itself in your behaviors. Remember, you cannot fix something that makes you fearful if you are unaware of it.

When we think of how fear affects the mind, most of us might think of the "fight-or-flight" response, which originates in the amygdala and then, after a complicated change in our bodies, the prefrontal cortex and hippocampus evaluate whether the perceived threat is real (Javanbakht and Saab 2017).

Fear triggers stress responses, releasing hormones like cortisol and adrenaline, which increase heart rate and blood pressure, preparing the body for fight-or-flight responses. This can lead to chronic stress if the fear is persistent, affecting overall health and well-being (Javanbakht and Saab 2017). In my personal example about growing up around drug addiction, I spent a lot of time in this fight-or-flight mode. Cortisol had to be flowing in huge amounts. I was super intentional about making myself move back into the prefrontal cortex in my thinking and in my decisions. Often, I talked myself off the ledge of self-pity and into a more rational and self-reliant way of thinking and then being.

Another impact of fear is cognitive biases, whether as confirmation or negative biases. Fear amplifies the tendency to focus on negative outcomes or threats, which can disproportionately influence one's perception and decision-making. This bias is well documented in psychological research, highlighting how individuals with heightened fear responses are more likely to perceive neutral situations as threatening (Bar-Haim et al. 2007). This negative bias is what makes me steer clear from well-known addictive drugs, but also from almost all drugs unless there is no other way around them. I am a work in progress in this regard. This is important for me to know, because our responses to others and circumstances in our environment could be latent with negative bias, which can distort our interactions and the realities around us.

Confirmation bias in everyday life is easy to see. We see this at a basic level when we are shopping for cars. You want a silver Honda Pilot and now you see them everywhere you go. They were there before, but you only noticed them when you fixed that possibility in your head. When fearful, people often seek information that confirms their fears, ignoring contradicting information. This can reinforce existing fears and lead to erroneous conclusions about the nature of the threat or the appropriate responses to it. This can be a real detriment to our ability to lead ourselves well, because we may perceive our world in completely inaccurate ways (MacLeod and Mathews 2012).

We all have some sort of bias. Do you want to guess what we need to improve to begin to make our biases work for us and not against us? Yes, self-awareness. Let us review methods to identify and overcome your fears, starting first with self-awareness.

Addressing and Overcoming Your Fear

I wrote extensively about self-awareness in Chapter 1, because it is by far the most important state of being we can focus on to grow in self-leadership. When it comes to overcoming our fears, we have to be aware of them and how we feel about them, how we

When you know the origins of your fears, you can begin to understand the ways they might be holding you back.

respond to them, and so on. At the end of this chapter, I will provide a few self-awareness exercises, specifically related to your fears. When you know the origins of your fears, you can begin to understand the ways they might be holding you back.

Before I decided to quit my job and start my own business, working with organizations on how to improve their customer and employee experience, I was burning the candle at both ends. In other words, I waited too long to take the leap into entrepreneurship, and my emotional well-being was declining. Being the breadwinner at the time for my family of six, I was afraid to leave and start my own consultancy because I wasn't quite sure that I could make enough to feed and care for them. Health insurance was a big sticking point. But at some point I realized I couldn't do it all. I began to see and feel the negative impacts of spreading myself so thin. I felt the anxiety and exhaustion take hold. Luckily, my consulting and training business was bringing in the same amount of income as my day job. I grew confident with the results I could see. While I was a little nervous, most of my fear began to melt away because I felt deeply that this was the work I was meant to do. I also knew that I would lose my sanity if I kept at the same pace trying to do all the things well.

In what ways could you give a new change in direction a try without going full in? Could you potentially be like me and grow in confidence just by starting and then allowing the results to drive you to take a bigger leap later? Are you listening to your emotional state and allowing that to guide you too?

One of the things many of us lose sight of is that we are not in the thing called life alone. In many ways, we are a community of people on a journey and encountering fear and setbacks along the way. Because of this, it is critical that you open up a dialogue with others about your fears in certain areas. When you do this, you help others see they are not alone, and you give them permission to do the same. Seek out a coach, mentor, or even a close friend to be a sounding board and help you think through whether or not your fears are worth the worry and what you can do about them. The "Bright Ideas for Self-Leadership" section below offers some mindfulness exercises to help you mitigate the fears you do have by helping you understand them and then putting them in their proper place.

One other thing I need to mention is that a great antidote to fear is preparedness. That old saying "When you fail to prepare, you prepare to fail" is true in so many ways. We often want certain results out of our personal and professional lives but don't put in the work to get to our desired results.

Honestly, I am more of a go-with-your-gut type of person who believes in rapid iteration just as much. But I have found that in the times either when stakes are high or I feel the most fear or nervousness, preparedness is the thing that calms me and centers me most.

My keynote speaking experiences are a part of the work I do around workplace culture and leadership. Even though, I am preparing to deliver a talk that I have delivered hundreds of times before, I do get nervous and sometimes have fear of flopping. Just because I speak from stages often does not mean I do not get nervous or sometimes have a fear of flopping. I do. The best antidote to all of those emotions is to prepare. When I prepare, I can be more present with those in the audience. When I prepare, I can show up as my whole self. When I prepare, I can deliver the exact message I am there to deliver to those who need to hear it. Think of preparation as something within your control and a great tool to counter the fears you have. You do not have to live in fear or allow your fears to take control of your ability to lead yourself with much more confidence and determination.

Bright Ideas for Self-Leadership

Fear Mapping (based on techniques from cognitive behavioral therapy)

Objective: Identify specific fears and their triggers.

Create a visual map of your fears (see Figure 3.1). Start with a central node labeled "My Fears." Draw branches for each fear you can identify, and from each of those branches, draw smaller branches that represent when and where each fear shows up in your daily life. This could include specific situations, thoughts, or feelings that trigger the fear.

Historical Reflection (work of psychologists such as James Pennebaker)

Objective: Trace the origin of each fear.

For each fear identified in the Fear Mapping exercise, write a brief narrative about the first time you remember experiencing this fear. Try to recall details about the situation, your age, other people involved, and how you felt. This reflection might reveal patterns or past experiences that have contributed to the development of these fears.

FIGURE 3.1 Fear mapping.

Personal Growth and Sustainability

Once we get much clearer about who we are and what we are meant to do with our lives, we are ready to focus on growing from there. Yet personal growth is not a destination, but a journey, and to sustain a growth mindset requires effort, grace, and resilience. In this part of the book we will focus on what is required to keep evolving and bring the GROW framework for self-leadership to the forefront.

4

Deciding Between Progress and Perfection

Often, we focus on getting things just perfect before taking risks, or moving forward for fear of it not being "just right." But self-leadership is much more about continuous improvement than any unattainable ideal of perfection. In fact, if you want to choose perfection over progress, you are quashing your opportunity to lead yourself in any effective way, or get results that you are seeking in your personal and professional life.

I have never been a person who expects perfection from myself in advance of attempting a task or a goal, but I am someone who pokes and prods about ways I could have approached a task in a different and better way. Sometimes, I over-evaluate my performance and kick myself around with the ways it wasn't this or that. But then I mentally shake myself back into the reality of what I know about all human beings. We are perfectly imperfect, and I am good with this. In fact, I have developed into an iterator, which is just someone who believes that it's possible to make something better but is comfortable knowing that a thing they have produced or accomplished is not perfect from the start. When I choose to see myself as an iterator, it opens my mind to accept that my creation is a journey. Some are comfortable with this approach; others are not.

Iteration might not be the most effective method in something like engineering where they are testing a result and need to try it over and over again to ensure the same result. I am not an experiment and, ideally, I do not want the same results as always. I am iterating to get a different, more evolved result, not a perfect result.

It's time to dive a little deeper into some of the pitfalls of perfection.

The Pitfalls of Perfectionism

Trying to be perfect holds you back more than you may think. Let's talk about how this would show up when interviewing for a better job. This pressure to compete for a single position or one particular type of recognition is put on display in the workplace when a more senior spot becomes available. Many people want this position, but only one person can have it. In this scenario, we go in to interview for it, and then we do not get the position. The thoughts start to pour in. We start to rewind the entire process in our minds and then we kick ourselves for not being or sounding "perfect." We think that this lack of perfection is what stopped us from getting that promotion. Realistically, you do not know why you didn't get the position. You could've said things a million different ways and still not gotten it. Beating yourself up for not being perfect is the wrong way to think about it.

There is a difference between a healthy striving for excellence and very counterproductive perfectionism. Here are the most common signs that you may be a perfectionist:

There is a difference between a healthy striving for excellence and very counterproductive perfectionism.

- You have very high standards. And sometimes those standards are too high for any one person to achieve.

- You thrive on organization and structure. And there are many times when this is not possible.

- You are very ambitious about your goals, which makes you strive and work harder. It can be a good thing, but then it also increases the pressure.

- You have difficulty getting over small mistakes and this is because you expect perfection in everything you do. This is an elusive concept, and even the best performers, athletes, and professionals make mistakes. It's what you learn from them that makes the difference.

- You are prone to procrastination, because you are so focused on the result that you cannot focus on the process you need to take to achieve the thing you want to achieve. Then you may feel guilty for delaying what is required (Cleveland Clinic 2023).

Being a perfectionist and striving for excellence can sometimes seem like one and the same, but the differences can be found by asking yourself the following questions:

- How do I react to mistakes? Do I see them as opportunities for learning and growth, or do they cause me significant stress and self-criticism?

- Do I feel satisfaction from my achievements, or do I struggle to acknowledge them, instead focusing on tiny mistakes?

- Are my standards achievable and realistic or are they unattainably high?

- How does pursuit of my goals impact my well-being, relationships, and overall happiness? Does it enrich my life or make me more anxious?

Answering these questions for yourself can help you decipher whether or not you are a perfectionist. If you really want to go deeper you can also take the perfectionist test on the *Psychology Today* website (http://www.psychologytoday.com/us/tests/personality/perfectionism-test). No matter which way you go, just know that your decision to choose progress over perfection will help you feel much better about the journey you're on.

Did you know that being a perfectionist can be bad for your mental health, and even for team dynamics? Yes, it can overlap, or even cause mental health conditions like obsessive compulsive disorder (OCD), eating disorders, social anxiety, and an overall reduction in feelings of self-worth (Cleveland Clinic 2023). That harsh inner critic we learned about in the previous chapter can fuel our desire to be perfect and of course we never arrive there. This strong need for perfect outcomes can also affect workplace relationships because it might extend to those with whom we work. If they do not complete a task just right, how hard do we come down on them? Do we allow them their mistakes?

When I was younger, I did take what I saw as "failures" hard, but not until I had my own children did I let my foot off the gas a little on my professional ambitions and my need to reach goals. As my kids reached different milestones, we would get giddy and celebrate with them and in our own minds. I realized that the steps we take are more important than how

The steps we take are more important than how large those steps were.

large those steps were. It became less about competing to reach bigger milestones faster and more about appreciating even the smallest of achievements. Embracing progress is the best way to feel good about who we are, where we're at, and where we're going. It's impossible to grow in self-leadership without this viewpoint.

Embracing Progress

Stan, an executive vice president at a bank, was debating whether to apply for a promotion for one of the coveted president spots at his bank. As I worked with him I could see his reservations about putting his name into the hat for the position, partly because he wasn't sure he had what it took to succeed in the role and partly because he wasn't sure if others would see him as possessing the skills necessary to do well in the role. We talked a bit about progress versus perfection and how he should see the interview for the position as just one more step in his career journey, not as his very last opportunity to achieve this position. There would be other opportunities that would come up. So even if he didn't get the position, just expressing his interest was a good step to take. This removed some of the pressure on his shoulders regarding his performance in the interview. In the end, he didn't get the position, but he knew he did his very best and he felt honored to have been asked to interview in the first place. For him, that was enough for the moment. He recognized the progress in his journey and did not get lost in the result.

Progress is a way of moving forward, when the pluses are more than the minuses in our life. If you pause for a moment to recall our definition of self-leadership as "the journey of growing inwardly to shine outwardly, spiraling upwards through self-awareness, resilience, and purposeful action," you'll see

> *Progress is a way of moving forward, when the pluses are more than the minuses in our life.*

that it's all about progress. The focus on progress inside ourselves helps us create long-lasting progress outside ourselves. Understanding this truth is critical to our personal and professional success. A huge part of this is recognizing and celebrating the small wins in our life. Truthfully, celebrating small wins can be a real sticking point for me. I often feel like I have so much to accomplish and not enough time to slow myself down to appreciate those wins. Then I think about why I'm so driven to do more and accomplish so much.

Do you remember my opening story in the introduction about attending a retreat to achieve certain results in my speaking business for 2024? The same place I learned about the Golden Buddha? On the opening night of that retreat, the host moved around the room and stood by each attendee to describe each person and what they spoke about. When it was my turn for him to describe me, his introduction hit me like a ton of bricks! At first, I was kind of irritated, because he described me much differently than how he described everyone else. As the retreat went on, the words he used to talk about me kept tossing around in my head. "Heather is the most competent person I have ever met. She gets shit done and does so much." Then, pausing for a moment, he looked at me, touched my shoulder, and said, "You know you do not have to do it all, right?" He continued, "She and her team get stuff done and she shows them that she cares for them while they do it. She is also an amazing mother who deeply cares for her children. I highly respect her for that." Then he moved on to the next person. I thought, "Wait a minute, why didn't you tell them what I speak about, and talk about my work from the stage?" By the next day, and after I heard that second recollection of the Golden Buddha story, it was all clear for me. Why did I do so much? Why was I now known as the "most competent person" anyone could know? Did I want that reputation? Is that how others perceive me? Do I want this kind of life where I am doing so much? Have I taken the right amount of time to recognize the wins along the way?

Then I set out to commit to *not* taking on more than was necessary, opening up my mind to the possibility that doing just enough was more than enough for me and my family. I also realized much of my drive stems from my origin story of not feeling good enough and being excluded early on in my life. That environment created in me a deep desire to do all I could do to be "good enough." I did not realize how embedded that thinking was in who I was and how I showed up.

After uncovering this truth about myself, I have been going out of my way to celebrate the small wins in me, my team, and my family. I would guess that those closest to me sometimes feel smothered by how my own personal drive extends to how I treat them, relate to them, and what I expect from them. I am now much more intentional about pausing more, evaluating how I'm feeling about their setbacks and not pressuring them to solve for those setbacks in a way that I used to do. I am slowing things down a bit to appreciate the little things and the little signs. For me, this evolved way of thinking and being provides room for others around me to grow and learn more than before. Does this resonate with you? Are you racing to an undefined finish line, or are you appreciating your journey to gradual betterment? Daily, I am aiming at the latter.

In Chapter 9, I will delve deeper into having a flexible mindset, but it's worth touching on the need to adopt a "growth mindset," a term coined by author and psychologist Carol S. Dweck, PhD, when looking at progress over perfection.

We often struggle to value our progress because we have, as Dweck calls it, a "fixed mindset," where "people believe their basic qualities, like their intelligence or talent, are simply fixed. They spend their time documenting their intelligence or talent instead of developing them. They also believe that talent alone creates success – without effort" (Dweck 2006). People with this type of mindset find it hard to see or celebrate progress, because deep down they do not really think you can show progress, since you are who you are.

On the other hand, Dweck advocates for a different sort of mindset, where people believe that their most basic abilities can be developed through dedication and hard work – brains and talent are just the starting point (Dweck 2006). For example, a student who holds a growth versus a fixed mindset has a significantly more positive learning experience, because they see their setbacks as opportunities to try again and improve. You can see, then, that it will be much harder for you to embrace progress if you see who you are, the skills you possess, and what you are able to accomplish as fixed in time and space with no ability for you to impact it. You would give up after you fall down and feel virtually powerless as the person you are today without considering who you can develop into tomorrow. Adopting and sustaining a growth mindset is crucial to growing in self-leadership, because how can you grow inwardly if you lack the belief in your ability to change and get better?

One of the things to consider or even lean into when trying to get better at embracing progress is to find simple and creative ways to measure your progress in your skills, projects, and even team achievements.

If you are in a management position, you could use a tool like a 360-degree feedback assessment when you get feedback from an extended group at work on your strengths and areas of opportunity. Then you can request to administer that annually to track your growth and progress. Any of us can find skills assessments and track how many new skills we're adding. LinkedIn offers skill tags that correspond to their course offerings as well. If you manage projects, you can create a project plan with the team and come up with milestones to be sure you're on track to complete the project on time. There are a plethora of ways to make sure you are progressing on any journey.

In December 2023, I embarked on a new health journey with a health coach. The year before, my doctor had told me that I was prediabetic and suggested I lose a little weight and watch what I ate. Honestly, I wasn't surprised. I had allowed myself too much grace and flexibility eating whatever I wanted from October to the end of February the year before. The advice of "lose a little weight and watch what you eat" sounds straightforward, right? Well, there was the goal to follow his advice and then there was getting it done. That's where my health coach came in. She helped me establish the habit of daily tracking of what I ate and drank. I would weigh myself daily and send the scale reading to her, and even packed my scale on trips to keep myself accountable, and it worked! I followed her advice, learned what to eat when, and what to stay away from. I learned to balance living my real life with my need to stay healthy. While the significant weight loss was wonderful, those new habits that focused on tracking my progress and tweaking along the way to improve my results will stay with me for a lifetime. And the good news about my next doctor's follow-up is that I am no longer prediabetic! It all happened fairly quickly (three months in total), and while some days were harder than others, I did it.

My efforts in this area also helped me see the importance of more closely tracking my professional endeavors as well. My work with the health coach also made me realize that I needed to set realistic goals so that I could feel successful early on.

Setting Realistic and Aspirational Goals

Once you make up your mind that progress over perfection is the only way to go, you need to focus on setting realistic goals that, when reached, make you feel successful and move you closer to your definition of success.

You may have heard of the famous SMART goal concept (specific, measurable, achievable, relevant, and time-bound). While I like the acronym, I think there might be a simpler way to set goals that could get us to our end goal faster and with more gusto and pizazz. Let's adopt a new way of setting goals using what I call the "ARC Method." It's shorter and has a level of stretching and inspiration embedded in it that I find lacking in the SMART goal concept. Here is how the acronym breaks down:

- **A** stands for Aspirational Vision. You must first start by envisioning your desired future state or outcome. Think big and dream audaciously about what you want to achieve. This is the good stuff that gets you out of bed on tough days. It lights a fire in your soul a much more compelling way. You want to be sure to define this vision in vivid detail, capturing the emotions, the experiences, and the impact you hope to create. Then ask yourself: What does success look and feel like? What is my ultimate dream? Just writing this gets me excited!

- **R** stands for Realistic Pathways. Once you come up with the aspirational vision, you will need to break it down into realistic pathways or strategies for achievement. Identify the specific steps, actions you will take, and resources you will need to move closer to your goal. Be sure to evaluate the feasibility of each pathway, considering factors like time, resources, skills, and potential obstacles. Then ask yourself: What are the most viable pathways for achieving my aspirational vision? What concrete steps can I take to progress toward my goal? This is when we start to make things happen. Things start to crystallize. You can begin to see the fruits of your hard work.

- **C** stands for Continuous Adaptation. If you have understood anything I have written so far, you know I believe strongly in continuous improvement and iteration. In this last step of the ARC Method, you want to embrace a mindset of continuous adaptation and flexibility as you work toward your goal. Recognize that circumstances might change, and adjustments might be necessary along the way. That's okay. Stay open to the possibilities, opportunities, feedback, and learning experiences that can inform your journey.

We will talk more about this way of being in Chapter 9 on flexible thinking and being. In the meantime, ask yourself: How can I adapt and pivot in response to changing circumstances or feedback? What lessons can I learn from setbacks?

This method of setting goals combines the realistic with the aspirational. It can keep you both grounded and a little dreamy, which, in my opinion, adds more excitement to our personal and professional path. In fact, I'd venture to guess that others will be inspired by us because we approach our goals with more passion and focus. Now, rather than feeling robotic, the goal-setting process inspires us to achieve at higher levels and elevates our self-leadership.

Remember, too, that adaptation is a critical part of this process. Do not confuse it with failure. Embedded in that word "failure" is a sense of giving up or lowering the bar on our expectations for ourselves. Adaptation says you can be fluid depending on the circumstances. Perfect represents a state of doneness that can never be found in an adaptable person. I can guarantee you that in the workplace,

> *Perfect represents a state of doneness that can never be found in an adaptable person.*

you will advance more in your career if you learn to adapt than if you learn to be "perfect." If you are adaptable, you will learn and grow from your setbacks much faster as well.

Learning from Setbacks

Among the various aspects of self-leadership, I believe the most critical one is the ability to promptly recover from setbacks encountered in the pursuit of one's goals and vision. It is awfully hard to shine outwardly if inwardly you are a hot mess with no clear path to get better. Setbacks, challenges, obstacles, and barriers are common in our personal and professional lives. We need to expect them, and even look for them if we want to grow in self-leadership. They build character. They enable you to transform from a diamond in the rough to a beautiful and brilliant jewel. When you think about the Golden Buddha story (the introduction in this book), its brilliance wasn't obvious until its outer surface of clay was cracked. That's when everyone could begin to see the shine, the value, the worth.

I have had some setbacks and challenges in life, one of them being the rejection by my family that I described earlier. But over the years, I decided that it was their loss that they chose not to be around me more. I made up my mind that I would be better than my family.

I went to law school – to this day the only one to do so on either side of my family. I stood tall and spoke well, and while I still wasn't included, it did not matter, because I had become my own advocate, as well as (by that point) an advocate for others who did not have a voice.

You see, I had a choice. I could live my life walking in my past, or I could use my past as the fuel I needed to exercise my hard-earned resilience muscle and help others do the same. I chose the latter.

What I see all too often are people inside and outside the workplace getting stuck in their own minds, in their own current circumstances, so much so that they cannot move forward.

The first and most important skill for anyone to have right now is the ability to intentionally think differently and reframe our current circumstances. Reframing is not a new concept, but it is being intentional about the reframing process that can make the difference in your personal and professional life.

To reframe an experience means to see it differently by replacing irrational thoughts and limitations with more rational thoughts that help you see your circumstances in a new light.

To reframe an experience means to see it differently by replacing irrational thoughts and limitations with more rational thoughts that help you see your circumstances in a new light.

Here are the steps to easily learn and remember how to reframe:

1. Acknowledge the irrational feelings and thoughts you might have for a period of time.

2. Give yourself a cutoff for how long you will rest in those thoughts. So you must acknowledge them as any human should, but then it must end (I call this the switch). Think of a switch that is in your mind, and you get to choose when to turn it on or off. In this case, you must turn off the switch of irrational thoughts.

3. Then set out to replace the irrational thoughts and feelings with rational ones that help remove some of the emotion.

4. Finally, you can repeat this as often as those thoughts or words surface.

I talked earlier about how I had to reframe the adversity in my life and find a way to move past it. While I had plenty of irrational thoughts as well as valid emotions around how I was treated as a child, I knew that I could not live in my victimhood if

I was to achieve great things. I had to get unstuck. I had to focus on moving forward and looking forward. I knew I was stronger for it all.

Some years ago, I was laid off from my job for the first time ever. It was an especially hard challenge because I was the main financial provider in my home. I was shocked to get the news and left there to go to my church and talk to my pastor. I was crying and I was a mess.

The thoughts that raced through my mind?

- How would I ever be able to pay for my children's tuition?
- Could I pay my mortgage?
- Would we lose our home and have to move?
- Would I even be able to find a new job?

These were all irrational thoughts that were founded solely on emotion and not grounded in facts, but I was stuck there, and I could have stayed there forever.

I allowed myself to acknowledge the fear and rejection for a few weeks. Then I had a change of heart, or a change of mind. I flipped the switch in my head away from thoughts that made me feel like a victim of my circumstances. After thinking about it more rationally, I realized several things: I learned a lot there and made some wonderful friends. Without the layoff, I would not have discovered what I was supposed to do – which is what I am doing right now!

I reframed all the previous negative and emotionally heavy feelings with ones that empowered me, and helped me to focus on moving and looking forward. I realized that there is no power in victim thinking, but really just the opposite. I replaced those irrational thoughts with more rational ones.

What words, thoughts, feelings, or stories are circling in your mind, and perhaps even flowing into your conversations with others?

Some examples of negative phrases we might find ourselves thinking or using include:

- "I have to."
- "I cannot."
- "This is impossible."
- "They control that."
- "Why does this keep happening to us?"

These are limiting thoughts, irrational thoughts that are purely emotional.

Now, I'm not saying that your current reality or circumstances are perfect or something to celebrate all the time. What I am saying is that how we think about our circumstances and the words we use to describe them greatly impact our course of action and our success in overcoming it.

The thing to focus on right now is what we *can* control and influence.

- Do not spend time on the things that don't concern you, but on those that you can influence or control. This hearkens back to what I said earlier in that we can control how we think and talk about our circumstances, and we can influence how others see it as well.

- The more you use limiting or victim-sounding words, the more you limit your influence and impact.

- The less you use those words, the more you expand what is possible and what you influence.

Do your thought patterns or habits move you forward or propel you backward? Write down the irrational words or thoughts that you have been using lately that could be holding you back.

Another important strategy to help build resilience in others is the idea of focusing on a mission that is bigger than yourself. I like to think of this like a bull's-eye, and when you keep your eyes on it, you do not miss the center as often.

My "bigger mission" is to give people a voice, teach others how to show more care for themselves and others, and help people feel like they belong at work.

In his book, *Leader of the Pack*, Matt Sweetwood chronicles his real-life experience living with an abusive spouse and the trauma she put their kids through. Matt describes a turning point as the father of the family when he is at work and his wife calls him very upset at herself for having done something terribly wrong to one of their five children. Matt described how he feared the worst as he raced home. When he walked in to see one of their children with blood coming down his head after his mother hit him with a coffee mug, Matt said that he reached a place where he realized he had allowed himself and his family to be unhealthy in many ways. He realized that he had to do things differently to get them to a better place. He went out of his way to separate himself and his children from their abusive mother. He took steps to make them feel safe again.

When I interviewed Matt on my *Leadership With Heart* podcast, I asked him how he did that. He explained, "I focused forward. I kept moving and put one step in front of the other." Wow! It sounds so simple, right? In what ways do we overcomplicate the obvious solutions to the things that are in our way? Matt's "bigger mission" was his family's safety, happiness, and overall well-being. That was the most important thing. He could focus on just that and bring it to life.

When we learn how to focus on a bigger mission, it will make overcoming any irrational fears or even facing real obstacles easier to bypass. The impact is minimized by doing this.

When we learn how to focus on a bigger mission, it will make overcoming any irrational fears or even facing real obstacles easier to bypass.

Remember, resilience is having the ability to recover quickly from tough circumstances. You have to practice this, meaning you have to be faced with tough times or challenging circumstances often before you get good at it.

Bright Ideas for Self-Leadership

Set realistic goals with the ARC Method

- Aspirational Vision: Envision your desired future outcome in vivid detail, capturing emotions and impact.

- Realistic Pathways: Break down your vision into achievable steps, considering time, resources, and potential obstacles.

- Continuous Adaptation: Stay open to adjustments and learning experiences along the way, embracing flexibility as circumstances change.

Reframe Setbacks with Rational Thoughts

When faced with challenges or setbacks, acknowledge irrational feelings and thoughts, then consciously replace them with rational ones. Reframing empowers you to move forward and focus on solutions rather than dwelling on obstacles.

Focus on a Bigger Mission

Define a mission that is larger than yourself, such as helping others or making a positive impact. Keeping your eyes on this bigger mission can provide clarity and motivation to overcome obstacles and stay resilient in the face of adversity.

Embrace Iteration Homework

Choose a project or task you have been hesitant to start due to fear of imperfection. Commit to starting the project with the mindset of iteration. Document your progress and any improvements you make along the way. Reflect on the process at the end of the week, noting how embracing iteration influenced your approach and outcomes.

5

Prioritizing Self-Care

I used to think of self-care as an event to be marked on my calendar, or one thing I did for myself that would make me feel better and less stressed in the moment. After years of holding that mainstream belief and still feeling exhausted, I knew I had to see self-care in a more holistic way. Did I mention I have four children? They taught me that I could not be the best mom I could be for them without first caring for myself. This is at the foundation of self-leadership. We must understand that at the forefront of leading ourselves is a way of being that prioritizes us in daily ways. If we are to be strong self-leaders, we need to learn to let go of the way everyone else thinks of self-care, and learn to lean in hard to a more expansive view.

It's important to know and own that self-care is a necessity for sustained personal and professional performance, not a luxury that we treat like an occasional add-on in our lives. In this chapter we are going to talk about different strategies for exercising self-care and the role of self-grace and self-forgiveness in the context of learning to lead ourselves well.

The Spectrum of Self-Care

The World Health Organization defines self-care as "the ability of individuals, families, and communities to promote health, prevent disease, maintain health, and cope with illness and disability with or without the support of a health worker." Although there are many other definitions, I like this one, because of its holistic and long-term view. I also truly appreciate that we can do this by ourselves and with the help of others. The underlying message in this definition is that we don't have to do self-care alone (World Health Organization n.d.).

There are many different components to self-care and all have personal and professional applications. In the last few years I really homed in on all components. I used to have an Apple Watch, but I lost it on vacation a few summers ago. I thought about purchasing another one, but I didn't really like the fact that I was so connected all the time with alerts. I already felt tied down to the buzzes from my phone. Instead, I decided to purchase the Oura Ring, which turned out to be the best decision I could make. Since wearing this ring, I am much more aware of my sleep patterns, stress, body temperature, and the impact of exercise on my overall readiness and heart rate. I love it, because it looks like a cool piece of jewelry, but it also helps me take care of myself. Most people have no idea that it's doing all of this for me, especially since it does not come with the pesky alerts of a smartwatch.

What I appreciate most about using this type of technology is that it serves as a passive source of my health information. I wake up feeling sleepy and then I realize I ate too late or drank a glass of wine too late, and it reminds me to change my habits so that I can wake up feeling more refreshed. Sometimes I see that my readiness score is low for a variety of reasons and choices I made the day before, such as choosing not to work out. Instead, I might focus more on rest, and a lower-stress type of day filled with hydration and sleeping. Our culture is so focused on being ultra-productive, which can often be counterproductive to our own health.

Recently, I woke up feeling horrible. I wasn't exactly sick, but I felt like I might be getting sick. I am at the beginning phase of perimenopause, and I could feel my stress level going off the rails. I had plenty to do that day, but I decided to sit outside in the sun in my driveway for a little while. I knew that I needed it and that my work could wait. My health could not. This is one of the key areas under self-care: *physical self-care*, which really focuses our minds on sleep, nutrition, exercise, and relaxation. In this example, I listened to my body enough to know that I needed to relax in the sunshine, which seems to melt away my anxiety.

I mentioned earlier in the book how realizing I was prediabetic set me on a path of wanting to be healthy, not just for me but for my four beautiful children. I owed it to myself to lean into my physical health with better nutrition, sleep, and more consistent exercise. For many years I've been someone who enjoys and finds great stress relief with exercise, but over the holidays I let my eating and exercise go downhill. I had a feeling my doctor's visit was going to come with bad news, but it was worse than I thought. It scared me into action, which inspired me to get serious about weight loss. By hiring that coach, I learned what it means to have balance in my eating and still maintain my significant weight loss and keep any talk of diabetes away from me.

One person I deeply admire for his consistent focus on physical self-care is Jon Acuff. Jon is a successful professional speaker who focuses a lot on goal setting and achievement, and he travels quite a bit. No matter what, he gets his run in. It wasn't always easy, but Jon figured out that he could start small. As he said,

"Running got a lot easier for me when I realized I didn't have to do it all at once. We love mottos like 'Go big or go home,' but the reality is that 92% of all resolutions fail because we tried to go big without a plan to build our way there. When I realized running hundreds of miles each year starts with running one at a time, I was able to stack up small wins every day" (personal communication, July 2, 2024). I really love this idea of taking it one mile at a time. When we release the need to do it all at once, we can actually begin to look forward to and enjoy the things that make our body healthier.

Have you had any of the struggles I've described around physical self-care? Have you met them with blame or indifference, or have you owned your journey and the results? Our roads to self-leadership are paved with imperfection, areas of growth and bits of enlightenment. When you focus on your own physical and emotional self, it makes you feel more alive and prepared to conquer what is in front of you at home or at work.

I had a great conversation with Sara, a busy professional communicator, and we spoke about her struggle with lupus. I found her mindset profoundly positive and empowering. We talked about how she often limits her activities so that she doesn't overly stress her body. She clearly understands what serves her body well and what does not. Sara shared about her intentionality about sleep, keeping active, and minimizing drinking alcohol. What was most interesting was her perspective on keeping the balance between protecting her health and preserving her joy:

> *Joy is medicine as well. Sometimes we choose to do the thing that might take our energy for the joy it brings us later on or the memories we get as a result. Even when I am on vacation with my husband and we have plans with friends, I excuse myself when it's time for me to go to bed, because I know it's the best thing for me. (personal communication, March 1, 2024)*

This little conversation with Sara hit me differently, because normally these decisions are presented as this or that, right or wrong. Sara helped me see that decisions about the different levels of our health aren't always straightforward. Often, we need to just make the choice whether or not the joy of the thing we are embarking on outweighs the potential physical impacts it might have on us. It's okay to make the choice on either side just as long as we are fully present for the consequences of our choices.

Sometimes, it's hard to separate the next component, *emotional self-care*, from the physical, since they really do build upon each other. It's difficult to talk about managing stress, cultivating a positive mindset, and dealing with things like workplace pressure without thinking of how we do this. Often, we do physical things to help us with our emotional health.

When I speak to audiences about Caring Leadership®, I always start with self-leadership and drill down into self-care. One of the things I impart to my audiences is that self-care can be small, consistent acts that make us feel grounded and reduce our stress. For example, if you are someone who loves to garden and feel at peace doing so, then bring a plant into your workspace, and when you are feeling extra stressed or approaching burnout, just go up to the plant and take a few deep breaths or even put the soil in your hands. This brings you back to your garden and back to that emotional balance.

Here are some other ways to really lean into emotional self-care and lead yourself more effectively:

- Take mental breaks throughout the day, like coloring in an art book, walking in the nearby park, or visiting the gym.
- Find hobbies outside of work, such as golfing, skiing, running clubs, or book clubs.

- Pursue professional development opportunities getting specialized certificates or improving your public speaking abilities.

- If working from home, throw a ball to your dog or cuddle your kitty.

- Find a coach or a therapist to help you grow and help you work through any potential mental health challenges.

I would be remiss if I didn't highlight the role of *spiritual self-care* when thinking about self-leadership. While I am a convert from Judaism to Catholicism, I am not necessarily saying you have to be religious to lead yourself well. Having some sense of spirituality can provide a deep sense of purpose and direction that you may be lacking overall or just in certain situations. For me, my faith provides a path forward for how I treat myself and others so that things like self-forgiveness and self-grace (which I will delve into later in this chapter) are embedded in my faith in very clear ways. Having said that, prior to my conversion, I already believed in these concepts, because I have been guided by them in a spiritual sense since I was a child. I hope my mentioning this here doesn't alienate anyone reading this. If you have read this far in this book, you know I believe in having an open and inclusive way of being that allows a space for others with differing views. While I am very clear about my personal values, it doesn't mean there isn't room for other views on this topic as well.

In what ways have you been guided by your own faith and spirituality? How have you grown or fallen short in spiritual self-care?

Now that we have looked at the three components of self-care, let's look at the real barriers to self-care and how to overcome them.

Overcoming Barriers to Self-Care

Have you ever worked at a company that "on paper" offers unlimited paid time off (PTO) or vacation, but then either no one ever takes it or they message you nonstop after you are on PTO, or there is an unspoken understanding that your career prospects are limited if you take "real" time off? This is one of the biggest workplace cultural barriers to self-care. We spend 40 hours or more at work each week. Often we are operating at such high levels of productivity that we might burn out. We need to take that time to decompress and focus on our own health, but sometimes the culture and the behavioral norms at work don't allow us to lean into that focus on us. For those in this type of work environment, here are some ways for you to take care of yourself despite the culture that you are in:

- Micro-breaks: Take short, frequent breaks throughout the day to recharge and refresh. This could be as simple as stepping away from your desk for a few minutes to stretch, take a walk, or practice deep-breathing exercises. Of course, if you aren't allowed to take these types of breaks, you might need to search for positions inside your current company or outside of it to be sure you have this time.

- Mindfulness practices: Incorporate mindfulness practices into your daily routine to reduce stress and increase resilience. This could include mindfulness meditation, mindful eating, or simply taking a few moments to focus on your breath and ground yourself in the present moment. Honestly, this is another weakness for me in my self-leadership. I have tried meditation a few times. I do remember being successful once when attending a conference where a facilitator did a wonderful job guiding us in meditation. I remember feeling so relaxed at that moment. I tried it on my own afterward and couldn't get to that state of calm, but I do know people who swear by this practice.

- Boundary setting: Establish clear boundaries between work and your personal time to prevent burnout and maintain work-life balance. Communicate your boundaries to colleagues and managers, and prioritize activities outside of work that bring you joy and fulfillment. I will write much more about this in Chapter 10, "Expect Clear Expectations." Embedded in this strategy is the idea of truly uncovering your boundaries so that you can be in the position to fight for them when they are compromised.

- Physical activity: Find opportunities to incorporate physical activity into your day, even if it's just a short walk during your lunch break or taking the stairs instead of the elevator. Regular exercise can boost mood, energy levels, and overall well-being. You will see this as a consistent theme throughout this book. The benefits that moving creates to your overall well-being and cannot be overstated.

- Connection and support: Seek out social connections and support networks within your workplace. Building relationships with colleagues who share similar values and interests can provide you with a sense of camaraderie and support during challenging times. I have learned to do this more and more, especially in more senior roles. There is a level of selective vulnerability when you manage other team members. They cannot be your safe space at work. Seek out colleagues at your level, or look into getting funding for a private coach. You might even consider using your organization's

Self-leadership doesn't mean you are doing life by yourself, but for yourself and with others.

employee assistance program (EAP) to just talk to someone regularly. Don't try to do it all – self-leadership doesn't mean you are doing life *by* yourself, but *for* yourself and *with* others.

- Creativity and expression: Make time for activities that ignite your creativity and bring you joy. Whether it's writing, painting, playing music, or engaging in a hobby, carving out space for creative expression can be rejuvenating and nourishing for the soul. My writing this book is a creative expression for me. I also like to use connect-the-dots books for adults and nature-based videos. I remember when my kids were young, I would take them on "Dora the Explorer" days to just take in nature with all its sounds, smells, and beautiful views. I would have them be on the lookout for worms, birds, and even just swaying trees and leaves making their way through the street in the stream of water pouring in from a neighbor washing their car. Seize the opportunity to open up that part of your mind to find the peace you need.

- Celebrate your wins: No matter how small, it is critical for you to celebrate even the smallest of wins or successes you have. As I write this book, I have a deadline that is just a few days away. While the journey is still long after meeting that first milestone, I need to celebrate the fact that I will have turned in my fourth book. In my wildest dreams, I never thought I would be a prolific writer. In college, I was an okay writer. I remember, midway through my college journey, my two favorite professors in political science both told me that I needed to take more writing courses to strengthen that skill. My ego was a little bruised, but I knew that I wanted to make them proud. They were amazing and really believed in me and my future. So I took those additional writing courses and moved from a B+/B− writer to an A− writer. I am not perfect, but I can celebrate that I put in the work and met their expectations and mine. Here I am today, continually writing books to help people around the world. This is no small thing, and we do need to also celebrate the small things. This is just one way to exercise self-care.

Aside from the cultural barriers that may be alive in your workplace, there are also personal barriers you create for yourself. I have found that many things that we think of as barriers aren't barriers at all, but opportunities. Let's look at this more closely.

Are there any beliefs or personal values that might be preventing you from prioritizing self-care? For me, I grew up with strong working women in my life. I remember my maternal grandmother working full-time well into her 70s. My mother has always worked very physical jobs in retail, rarely taking vacations. I just remember her working a lot! I don't remember ever not having "enough" of anything, but work and working for some other company was always at the center of my home life. My father worked in hotels as a stagehand, and he belonged to a trade union. I do recall him having to go on strike and marching on picket lines, which meant he would be out of work and not getting paid much at all. What I have come to understand is that many of our beginnings can help us make sense of why we think and behave the way that we do today. I also learned that the leaders around us show us what is acceptable by their actions much more than their words. So a "work hard, play hard" or a "take time for yourself" philosophy is not something I grew up with. I thought I needed to work as hard as I could to get what I wanted out of life. This meant putting in long hours and not putting in enough time to care for my personal health.

Not until my late 30s or early 40s did I begin to stop feeling guilty when I took time for myself. After being an only child in the environment I described earlier and now having four children in the span of seven years, I was worn down and had no clear path forward to exercise good self-care. It wasn't really until I experienced that panic attack that I described in Chapter 2 that I realized something had to change. I needed to become "the boss of me." At that point, I wasn't thinking of entrepreneurship in the traditional sense of "boss." I just needed to take ownership in my own workplace and life journeys. I had no one to blame and had all the power within me to make the necessary changes.

If I didn't begin to care for myself, to lead myself, I would be at the behest of someone else for my entire life.

Have you ever been here? Were your values and beliefs getting in the way of caring for yourself? I invite you to inventory your deep-down beliefs around work, self-care, and your power at work and in your own life. We have to understand this in order to overcome any beliefs that are creating barriers to leaning into self-care. Once we do, we can be clearer about the boundaries we need to set for ourselves. Yes, you read that right. Don't wait around for someone else to tell you your boundaries, but set those in advance and recalibrate what you need for yourself to feel centered and balanced and ready to lead yourself and then others. Then you can find the courage and energy to communicate your needs to others. That's when you will see your true power shine through and learn to lead yourself more brilliantly than you thought possible.

Case Study

Simone Biles: A Champion in Self-Leadership

There's no escaping the Olympic news surrounding Simone Biles. At the Tokyo Olympics, she shared a tweet hinting at her struggles with mental health. Simone thus began the narrative of what would soon become the focus of the world on Sunday, July 25, 2021, after the qualifying round:

> *it wasn't an easy day or my best but I got through it. I truly do feel like I have the weight of the world on my shoulders at times. I know I brush it off and make it seem like pressure doesn't affect me but damn sometimes it's hard hahaha! The olympics is no joke! BUT I'm happy my family was able to be with me virtually♡ they mean the world to me!*

Unfortunately, things soon got even tougher for Simone. Not long after, Simone withdrew from team finals, the all-around competition, and the first three event finals. The cause for her withdrawal? Her well-being and her mental health. As she said on social media, "For anyone saying I quit, I didn't quit, my mind and body are simply not in sync." She also said, "Physical health is mental health."

Astoundingly, at the Paris Olympics in 2024, Simone won four medals and hinted that she might not be done with the sport just yet. What an amazing example of resilience and self-leadership!

The Mental Health Epidemic   Simone Biles is a young woman who has faced adversity in many forms, beginning with growing up as an African American woman. (I can relate to the challenges that presents.) It's public knowledge that, while simultaneously starring on the largest virtual stage at the Olympics, Simone was also a victim of former team doctor and convicted sex offender Larry Nassar. When she said, "I truly do feel like I have the weight of the world on my shoulders at times," not even a part of me doubts that for a second. She may be renowned as the GOAT (greatest of all time), but she is first and foremost a human being. She taught the world a lesson in self-leadership at the Tokyo Olympics, and I thank her for that.

Self-leadership is of critical importance for the Caring Leader, in that if she doesn't lead herself first, she cannot properly care for those she leads. She must understand her purpose and why she leads; be self-aware and understand and adapt to the people around her; have control over her mindset; understand the role of influence; consistently grow her skills; have a coach or mentor; and simply take time to care for her mind, body, and spirit.

A True Leader and True Champion Simone Biles demonstrates true self-leadership in her exemplary self-awareness, with a depth of understanding that most people are too afraid to delve into when it comes to self-reflection. She exhibits resolute control over her mindset and extreme care for her teammates. She understands the role of her influence, but does not let the power of influence interfere with her knowledge of what was truly best for her. She takes a powerful stance as she stands up for the well-being of her mind, body, and spirit while bowing out of the competition.

Among the most basic needs of a human being, as proven by science, are safety and security. Just look at Maslow's hierarchy. Simone Biles has proven her prowess as a leader, not only in the sport of gymnastics but among the ranks of humankind when she took great care to maintain her own safety and security while under a huge amount of pressure.

Her decisions to withdraw from Olympic events and prioritize her mental and physical health demonstrate that she is just as much a leader off the podium as she is on it. And she is just as much a champion of her sport as she is a champion for mental health. Mental health is a challenge that nearly every human being will face at some point in their life, and that's infinitely more people than in the world of gymnastics.

Bright Ideas for Self-Leadership

Self-Care Assessment

Exercise 1: Self-Care Practices Review   Instructions: Take 15 minutes to complete the following self-assessment quiz. For each area, rate your current practices on a scale of 1–5 (1 = Poor, 5 = Excellent):

Self-care area	Rating (1–5)	Notes/Reflection
Physical well-being		
Emotional health		
Mental clarity		
Spiritual fulfillment		

Instructions: Download and explore these apps to support your self-care journey:

- Meditation: Headspace, Calm
- Exercise: MyFitnessPal, Nike Training Club
- Time Management: Todoist, Google Calendar
- Mental Health: Moodfit, Happify

Exercise 2: Engaging Prompts   Instructions: Reflect on these prompts weekly to stay engaged with your self-care journey:

- What self-care activity brought me the most joy this week?

  _____

  _____

- How did I manage stress this week?

  _____

  _____

- What new self-care activity would I like to try next week?

  _____

  _____

6

The Three Stages of Empowerment

I get really riled up when I hear people placing blame on the world, or on others for why they are where they are. I am further irritated when I see people *waiting for* someone else to give them permission, access, or the idea to take the best next step for their own benefit. In many ways, we have become unempowered people. That is why I decided to write this book. I want to challenge you, especially when thinking about self-leadership, to learn to empower yourself. Don't wait for someone else to do it for you. I'm not saying that you cannot ask for help when you need it or that there aren't factors out of your control or people who have more authority to decide things. I am saying that you can learn to sail your own ship, become your own captain, be the leader of you!

The majority of definitions for empower, empowerment, or empowered position are as a kind of "receiving" power from an outside source: a boss, a leader, a politician, a law. I want you to think of empowerment more as something that you do for you, first. You give yourself the power to decide what you will do in and for your personal and professional life. By extension, you decide, and thus own, your own professional and personal growth and development. I have seen this play out recently with a certification program I recently rolled out. Many of the facilitator applicants decided to enroll and become certified despite their employer not choosing to contribute monetarily. A small number declined when their employer wouldn't cover any of the costs. One could argue that the latter weren't in the position to pay on their own while the others were. I can tell you this is not that simple. I recall one of my facilitators hesitating at first because her budget was tight, but then she came back and decided to cover the entire thing herself. She decided to bet on herself and not wait for her manager or company to place that bet. She was empowered, not by someone else, but by her desire to have and to be more.

But how can we all become empowered like this? It's important to understand that there are stages of empowerment so that we can have more control over moving through them faster and arriving at the place of being empowered, and maybe even empowering others. The three stages of empowerment are the Awakening, the Struggle, and the Breakthrough (Figure 6.1). As we explore these stages in the next sections, listen to where you might be within them.

FIGURE 6.1 Empowerment in visualized stages.

Stage 1: The Awakening

I like to think of this first stage as the Awakening because we often need something or someone to jolt us out of our mummy slumber of living in complacency and the status quo. The first steps to ponder to fully awaken is to recognize your current state, your limitations, and even areas where you lack control.

Some years ago, I worked at a company that was merging five companies to create one brand. The current and new employees were not trusting one another; people with similar titles were hired and fear and mistrust took hold. I felt like a victim of my circumstances. I was afraid of what might happen and it was sending me into a pit of mental despair. But the fear smacked me into a state of awareness around my defeatist mindset, and I knew I had to do something about it. So I went to see the head of HR and told her that we needed to take control of the diminishing culture in our office. She agreed, and I agreed to lead the creation of a culture team to help bring more positivity into the office despite the fear and turmoil. I understood where we stood, and where I stood in the midst of the merger; I understood there was only so much I could control and I knew that I was limited in my abilities to stop it from happening. Having said that, the Awakening I experienced was profound, which is what led me to start that culture team.

What is your current state at work, or even at home? Are you being led predominantly by others? Have you ever documented or thought about the areas where you lack control and in the place you feel the most and the least empowered? These are all things to consider before thinking more deeply about whether you have a true desire to change from your current state.

When you think of the Awakening that is required to empower yourself, the next most critical area to look at is whether you have a desire to change. Any organizational change or personal

> *Without the will to be different or better, change can never be sustainable.*

change rests on a person's or a team's desire to change. Without the will to be different or better, change can never be sustainable. You cannot feel empowered today and unempowered tomorrow, because to be in a state of empowerment carries with it more of a long-term view. You might feel motivated from one minute to the next, but you will feel empowered and be empowered working with a leader, a team, an organization, or in your own skin for much longer. Your desire to change is a catalyst to living in a state of empowerment for much longer.

I know that change isn't always as easy as willing it into existence. That is why in the Awakening stage, we need to focus on new knowledge acquisition. Often, we need new information or a new way of seeing things to bring the change in us to life. This new information serves as a sort of scale or teeter-totter that requires us to actively engage in order to balance. Here are some ways to acquire new knowledge to move this process along:

- Educate yourself via podcasts, books, online courses, attending workshops, and seminars.

- Ask for feedback from friends, family, coworkers, coaches. This could include finding an accountability partner who you spend a lot of time with, telling them what you are working on, and enlisting their feedback. You could also look for a mentor.

- Exercise some of the self-awareness strategies you learned in Chapter 1.

- Join trade associations in your job field.

- Attend networking events with like-minded or not-so-like-minded people.

- If you are in a management position at work, request 360-degree feedback from those around you via your learning and development team.

Remember, change won't happen outside of you until you decide it needs to first take place inside of you. That starts with the Awakening and an awareness of what is currenting happening and what you can or cannot do about it. Then it moves on to what is absolutely necessary to get to the other side to a place of self-empowerment, and that is the Struggle stage.

> *Change won't happen outside of you until you decide it needs to first take place inside of you.*

Stage 2: The Struggle

As any of us set out to change and become more empowered, whether individually, as a team, or as an organization, there is bound to be resistance. There are internal and external factors that can challenge us to step outside of our comfort zone and to become truly empowered to be our best.

Fear of the Unknown

Fear of what lies ahead can be paralyzing, as the comfort of the familiar is replaced with the anxiety of the unknown. This makes the struggle very real even though much of it starts in our minds and we build it up from there. People often prefer the security of their current situation over the potential risks associated with change. I have to admit that I have been this person in the past. It took me quite a while to leave my safe and secure day job before I finally decided to take the leap into becoming an entrepreneur. I was comfortable with my lofty salary and great health benefits. It wasn't until I could feel my mental health slip and my sense of being centered fade when I decided that I could no longer rest in comfort. I decided to shake things up and lean into the discomfort of the unknown. Would I succeed as a business owner? Would I be able to pay my bills and provide for my family? Many questions and concerns oscillated in my head. The struggle was real, but I didn't let it stop me from making the empowered decision to chart my own course.

Resistance from Others

Besides the fear of the unknown, another area that might amplify our struggle is the resistance that often comes from others. Your family, friends, and colleagues may resist or discourage you to change due to their own fears or discomfort with the new situation. I have always heard that we shouldn't take advice from people who haven't achieved or weren't successful in achieving what we want to do. Self-leadership means that we fight against the need to let others determine our direction or approach. This includes things like societal norms and expectations regarding your need to maintain the status quo or to change in one way the other.

Often, you might feel shunned for making one decision to change direction in direct conflict with what others might want from you. I understand how it feels to experience resistance from others. When I decided to quit the practice of law to sell Mary Kay Cosmetics, my grandmother and my mother were stunned! They thought I'd be the lawyer of the family. I could have stayed on the path they wanted for me, but I would have been miserable. I chose to empower myself to make my own career decisions, and I haven't regretted that decision this many

We either learn to lead ourselves or someone else will happily step in to tell us what our life should be.

years later. We either learn to lead ourselves or someone else will happily step in to tell us what our life should be. I don't know about you, but that idea makes my skin crawl. Think about ways that you can bet on yourself and your own awareness of who you are and what you want.

Lack of Resources

When thinking about the Struggle to be empowered to make decisions regarding a particular change, sometimes you or your team might experience financial constraints, because many times change requires a financial investment. What I have found is that we think we need more than we do really need, because we build things up in our mind. When we release the need to start everything only when things are "perfect," we experience more success in our ventures. Another thing that can stop us in our tracks is a lack of time. At the ripe old age of 53, I have found that my time is my most valuable resource. Having said that, four children, a podcast, and a thriving business doesn't always open up time for new things or even new ways of thinking. We need to take time to allow creativity to flourish. When we spend too much time in the weeds of our lives, we stunt our ability to *do* anything better or different. As I age, I am much better about parsing out moments to think and be. Could you adopt a more open approach to how you use your time?

Lack of Skills or Knowledge

Sometimes we want to feel and be more empowered, but we lack the skills or knowledge to branch out into a new area. This also can create a steep learning curve that can make it hard to move past our current state to a more powerful place. This lack of knowledge can create in us a sense of insecurity, or even more of that imposter syndrome I wrote about in Chapter 1.

When I first started in my role with the company that would eventually go through that complicated merger and layoff, I was thrust into having to learn how to do product demos on a brand-new technology platform. I had never done this type of work before. I was a little nervous to take this on, but then again it was exciting to be doing something new and offering clients a new way to do business with the firm. While it was a learning curve for me, I became the main person training new people on how to conduct such demos for clients. It felt good to take on a new role and show myself that I could do hard things.

The solution: Get comfortable with the discomfort of trying something new. Acknowledge that it might be uncomfortable and chat with your team, manager, and family about the new thing you are embarking on and set ground rules for feedback and define the margin of error for setbacks that might happen while you work through the learning curve. You can do this!

Institutional Barriers

So you've decided you're going to take control of your decisions and move forward with new ideas at work, and then you run right into the bureaucracy and processes that stop you right in your tracks. It's common that the institutional barriers that make good companies run smoothly can also inhibit empowered thinking that supports moving outside of the status quo. For example, you might work in a highly regulated environment, where the laws may restrict the ability to make certain changes, or there could be an unspoken policy that is frowned upon if violated.

When I was hired to lead a massive customer experience overhaul, in my usual "take-charge" way I dove into interviewing staff, interviewing customers, and putting together a plan to make things move along in an inclusive way. Then I began to encounter roadblocks at every turn. Even though I was hired to do the job I set out to do with confidence and zest, the culture didn't allow for quick decisions or changes. To the contrary, things moved at a snail's pace, and I grew increasingly frustrated in the process. Over time. I found some ways to work around the obstacles in front of me, because I refused to give up on my work mission. The organization did not always like the speed with which I moved on initiatives and sometimes I could feel that resistance. I tried hard for it not to defeat my mindset. I refused to give my power away.

You might be in a similar position. Maybe you were hired to do a job and something stopped you from doing it according to your plan. Perhaps there is some policy that thwarts your ability to move forward a change initiative and get good work done. I promise you that if you don't mind, it won't matter. Said differently, commit to keeping the empowered mindset in place so the resistance you feel transforms into the opportunity you can seize.

Commit to keeping the empowered mindset in place so the resistance you feel transforms into the opportunity you can seize.

By understanding and addressing these challenges, you can increase the likelihood of successfully changing your status quo and exiting the struggle stage to arrive at the Breakthrough, which is where you come out more empowered, leading yourself first and then having more influence with others.

Stage 3: The Breakthrough

When I think of the Breakthrough, I can't help but visualize jumping into a beautiful ocean and swimming up and out to the beautiful sunshine! This stage is where true self-empowerment is obvious to us and to those around us. That power that is deep inside of us literally breaks through to the surface, and now we can really see the Art of Self-Leadership in full force. What is the impact of truly rising above the Struggle and being more empowered?

Following are some things to consider.

Sense of Autonomy

One of the most positive impacts of this stage is that you can achieve the autonomy that you need to lead yourself. When you arrive here you will feel a sense of control and self-determination to do what you set your mind to, despite someone else's perceived barriers. You no longer wait for access or permission, or even place blame on others for your current state, but commit to taking action to be the change you are seeking.

Realization of Potential

One of the things that stops us from leading ourselves well is that we fail to recognize and then realize our full potential. We might even overestimate someone else's abilities and minimize our own capabilities. As I began my more formal journey to professional keynote speaker, I hit a wall in recognizing what made me unique. I had a hard time identifying my capabilities on stage, but I would always see greatness in my speaker colleagues. It took me a solid year of practice and feedback from clients to recognize and then realize my potential. That's when the good stuff began to happen, because now I'm able to lean into my own brilliance and continue to elevate my potential with every choice I make that serves me.

Influence and Impact

An exciting byproduct of being self-empowered is that you can now better influence those around you and have a greater impact in the process. People begin to pay attention to what you say and what you do; they might even follow you down a certain path where before you felt unheard and unseen. When you focus on becoming an empowered person, it puts you in the driver's seat instead of being in someone else's car sitting in the backseat without any control. Have you ever noticed that in your life? It feels liberating to finally be someone of influence, doesn't it? Next, let's talk about what you can do to transition between the stages in a more intentional way.

Transitions Between Stages

I believe that thinking about empowerment in stages helps us come up with strategies to identify which stage we are in and how to transition between them. From the Awakening to the Struggle stage, you are transitioning from awareness that something has got to change to facing challenges head-on and cultivating a resilient mindset while you go about changing how you think, how you behave and the types of things you accept out of life, work, and relationships. The biggest indicator that you have made this transition is that things might feel a bit uneasy, out-of-control, and stressful, and you fight against the urge to give up.

From the beginning of the Awakening stage to the Breakthrough stage, there is usually a trigger and a turning point. In my example of my professional speaking career, the triggers that jolted my awareness that something needed to change were, first, my lack of clarity for myself, but also realizing that I needed to show up with a unique value proposition to my prospective clients. If I didn't gain clarity about what I brought to the stage, my client would have a hard time doing that as well. This meant that I would not get the types of engagements for which I was hoping. My turning point to help me break through the struggle to identify and leverage my unique and compelling approach was when clients began to use words in their testimonials that affirmed my new direction and recognized my unique gifts. This gave me more confidence to continue to march forward with the path that I chose. What are your triggers, and what is your turning point? Will you be more intentional with seeking out the signals to help empower you and lead yourself better? Let's dive into the ways to sustain this new way of being once you've arrived at the Breakthrough stage.

Sustaining Empowerment

So, now you are this incredibly empowered person who no longer waits to be told when you can and should do something. You make informed decisions from a position of strength and not fear and you know how to persevere in ways you feel are appropriate. But, how can you sustain this empowerment? How can you be sure you won't revert to your old way of being? Here are five strategies you can focus on to be sure that you stay the course:

Set and Achieve Goals

While I did not make up the term SMART goals (specific, measurable, achievable, relevant, and time-bound), I have used this method of goal-setting to achieve what I set out to do, with book-writing, my business, and even my physical fitness goals (Mind Tools Content Team n.d.). Breaking larger goals into smaller, manageable steps helps us stay motivated. We need some level of motivation to stay on track with being a more empowered person of influence. Also, don't forget about the ARC Method I shared with you in Chapter 4 if you are looking for a method that has more inspiration as its core.

One other thing that can sustain you is to focus on celebrating your wins. You have to acknowledge and recognize even the smallest achievements, because it will help reinforce your progress and build your confidence. I am getting much better at doing this. I tend to be someone who moves quickly and focuses on achieving the very next thing. However, I know that is not a good way to lead others or myself. I love recognizing even the smallest of wins for those who look to me in some way, yet I had a hard time doing that for myself, but no more! As I write this book, I know that I am strong and determined and amazing for setting out to write this fourth book with a life that is busier than ever. This is about impact. This is about you!

Continuous Learning and Development

If you want to sustain the Breakthrough stage, you need to commit to ongoing personal and professional development. I mention this a few different times in this book, and that is because this type of learning and development is your responsibility to yourself. There is no need to wait for a book or a human resources department to tell you when it's time to learn or grow. Identify areas where you want to grow and set specific, achievable learning goals and then load in some aspirational elements to keep you inspired. Remember, you are the boss of you.

Practice Self-Compassion

If you want to sustain an empowered way of being, you must be kind to yourself. You will need to learn to practice self-compassion, especially when faced with challenges or failures. Treat yourself with the same kindness and understanding you would offer a friend. Compassion is taking action to alleviate another person's pain, but you must take care of your own pain first. Honestly, this is a hard one for me. I have four children and I am an only child. To this day, I struggle with balancing my desire to be a great mom with my need to rest and relax for my own good. I can be hard on myself when things don't go well, but I was never focused on being the perfect mom. That would make me completely unrealistic and completely full of myself to think I could obtain

If you want to sustain an empowered way of being, you must be kind to yourself.

perfection. I practice self-compassion when I take time to pause, breathe, sit in the sun, lie in my tub, get a pedicure, pray, go for a walk, or simply do nothing. You can show yourself compassion too (Martin 2023).

Some months ago, I was traveling to the Poconos for a speaking engagement when the driver – let's call her Kathy – launched into a long and interesting conversation with me about the death of her late husband, who passed away at a young age from colon cancer. She was beautiful inside and out and you could tell she focused on both the inner and outer work to empower herself as a young widow and now a single mom. She confessed that while it was not easy living without him, she "wakes up every day happy" to do things that make her happy. She was emphatic that it was up to her to control her mindset and not wallow in the grief and the position she was in. She focused on listening to positive audiobooks and podcasts and reading often. She owned her own empowerment to take control of her life and live it to the fullest. I was impressed by her resilience as well. Maybe we can all learn a little from Kathy about moving past this Struggle stage with grace and sustaining an empowered mindset.

Build a Supportive Network

In my book *The Art of Caring Leadership*, I talk about the need to find a supportive network. Self-leadership is not synonymous with doing things all by yourself. This concept never goes out of style. If we want to lead ourselves well, we must surround ourselves with friends, family, mentors, and others who do not just tell us good things, but tell us hard things. These are people who are positive, and who encourage you and uplift you. Don't try to do this life on your own. This supportive group will help you see your blind spots.

> *Self-leadership is not synonymous with doing things all by yourself.*

Along these same lines, find mentors who can offer guidance, advice, and support as you navigate your personal and professional journey. I never had a formal mentor, but I have sought out the advice of many different people and used others as a sounding board when I am contemplating decisions.

Regular Review and Adjustment

Regularly review your goals, progress, and strategies. Adjust your plans as needed to stay aligned with your evolving aspirations and circumstances. Things will be consistently changing and evolving. If you remain status quo for too long, you will quickly find yourself going right back to the Struggle. This will happen anyway through life, but you want to be in control of when you move in and out of these stages as much as possible. I would recommend taking time to review your current state semiannually, by taking a day or a long weekend to review.

Bright Ideas for Self-Leadership

Reflection Prompts

1. Reflect on your current state at work or at home. Are you predominantly being led by others? Identify areas where you lack control and where you feel the most and least empowered.

   _____

   _____

2. Do you have a genuine desire to change your current state? Reflect on past experiences where you felt the need to change and what motivated you.

   _____

   _____

3. Reflect on a recent struggle you faced when trying to implement change. How did you overcome it, or what held you back? How did fear, resistance from others, or lack of resources play a role?

   _____

   _____

4. Think about a breakthrough moment in your life. What triggered this breakthrough and how did it change your perspective or actions?

   _____

   _____

Plan for Empowerment

Create a detailed plan for moving through the three stages of empowerment. Include specific actions you will take, resources you will use, and potential obstacles you may face.

Select one area where you feel disempowered and commit to learning more about it. This could be through reading books, attending workshops, or finding a mentor. Document your learnings and how they contribute to your empowerment.

7

Keying in on Your Strengths

In Chapter 1, I introduced the concept of intrinsic worth and the fact that you are good just by being on this earth. This chapter will focus us on uncovering, developing, and applying our strengths in the context of work. We must know ourselves in order to let ourselves shine through.

When we think about the time we spend at work, we want to be sure we are doing work that puts us in a position to shine, doing what we naturally do best. When we do work that helps us lean into our personal strengths, we find work more meaningful and have a better go at career success. I previously shared my personal story of how I uncovered my value by understanding my values. I also discovered what my strengths were and tried to apply those at every job where I was a team member. While I knew I could do some things better than others, I also discovered that there were areas where I could shine and even differentiate myself for promotions and leadership positions. This is why strengths-based development is so crucial for both individuals and organizations. You want to dig deep and do the homework to discover your strengths. If you manage a team or an organization, you want to also uncover the strengths of your people. That's how we achieve more, together!

Discovering Your Strengths

Regrettably, when I was in college, my campus leaders didn't promote or evenly openly provide personality- or strengths-based assessments to help students identify the best areas to pursue a career. I didn't have any of that available to me until much later. I just wasn't aware how important it was to pinpoint my strengths and then find work that promoted their use. These days, an unlimited number of assessments can help you discover your "special sauce," your "sweet spot," or the area or career field in which you can shine most. Following are some of my favorites.

DiSC

DiSC® is a communication and behavioral preference assessment that can help people understand their communication style and preferences. It measures strengths and areas needing improvement. When people see their tendencies, they can also see blind spots that stand in the way of team and career success. It increases self-awareness and awareness of the needs of those around you to help you form better relationships. Psychologist William Moulton Marston first detailed the behavior model in his 1928 book, *Emotions of Normal People*. His theory was that the behavioral demonstration of emotion could be categorized into four types: Dominance, Inducement, Submission, and Compliance. Marston theorized that a person's self-perception and understanding of their primary behaviors could help them better manage relationships and experiences. The four types have been modernized and changed to Dominance, Influence, Steadiness, and Conscientiousness, otherwise referred to as DiSC. I am a certified facilitator using this assessment. I like its practical use, and I think it really helps to understand what I need and then what others around me who have different communication preferences and styles need too. In the context of discovering your own unique talents and giftedness, this assessment can help you see how your specific way of communicating can bring out the best in others, potentially resolve conflicts more quickly, and land on solutions to everyday challenges with more ease.

DiSC® is a personal assessment tool used by over a million individuals annually to boost teamwork, communication, and productivity. By taking a 15–20 minute assessment, you'll receive a personalized profile detailing your unique behavioral style and strategies for effective interaction, followed by a 20-minute review with Heather R. Younger. This process helps drive lasting behavioral changes, positively impacting workplace dynamics.

Get started today: https://www.caringleadershiplearning
.com/DISC

CliftonStrengths

I took this assessment over 20 years ago, and then when I took it again recently my profile was mostly the same. I like it because it actually pinpoints your strengths. Clifton was an American psychologist and researcher who founded a company that later acquired Gallup Inc., where he became chairman and then developed this assessment. It is backed by research and has been taken by thousands across the globe. I asked my close friend

Sarah Elkins, who is a certified coach, to give me more background on this assessment and why it might help you lead yourself more effectively, and here is what she said:

> *What I love about this assessment is its value as a tool for healthy self-reflection. It's not a personality assessment – StrengthsFinder uncovers language to describe your natural, instinctive approach to problem-solving and relationship-building. Understanding our blind spots helps us manage them, but what some of us miss without significant self-reflection is the ability to use our talents to better support the people who can balance those blind spots for us. We can't be good at everything, and when we try, we end up being mediocre at most things. By understanding our talents at this level, we become better at team building, ensuring we surround ourselves with the right people, tools, and technology, so we spend more time in the pocket of our strengths while developing and valuing the strengths in the people around us. (S. Elkins, Certified Strengths Coach and author, personal communication, April 22, 2024)*

When we value the different talents others bring to the table, we strengthen our relationships, and we build their confidence and satisfaction at work. When we understand our own strengths in a clear way, we know how to promote ourselves better, ensuring better opportunities at work to shine.

Myers-Briggs

It's been almost 30 years since I took the Myers-Briggs assessment, which "is designed to help people identify and gain some understanding around how to take in information and make decisions, the patterns of perception and judgment, as seen in normal, healthy behavior" (www.myersbriggs.org). "The Myers-Briggs framework consists of eight preferences organized into four pairs of opposites." Any one person's type represents their natural preferences in four important areas of personality. Like DiSC, some people prefer one side of a preference pair over another, which accounts for the differences between different people (www.myersbriggs.org). It looks at things like extroversion and introversion and thinking and feeling. It creates a way to label ourselves and know which behaviors and thus which people we align with most closely. Like many other assessments, it helps us simplify the complex.

Any of these above assessments will help you gain a deeper understanding of your preferences, personality, and unique strengths. Then you will begin to remove the clay over your brilliance and others will see it.

360-Degree Feedback

About 10 years ago, I took my first ever 360-degree feedback assessment. They're usually reserved for senior managers in an organization, so I wasn't super familiar with it when my manager, then the CEO of the company, asked all of his direct reports to take it. Here is how it works: You gather a list of your direct reports, choose a handful of colleagues – and sometimes customers if you are customer facing – and then your direct manager completes it. They want to gauge how all of these groups perceive your strengths and areas of improvement. When you get your report, the only person you know for sure responded is your manager. You don't know who else responded or how they responded. You get to see only the aggregate feedback. Admittedly, my feedback was not all rosy and cheerful. In short, my direct reports loved me, my colleagues thought I spent way too much time recognizing people in the organization, and my manager seemed to think I was awful but the best of all his direct reports. In many ways, it was painful to read (more on this in Chapter 11). Nonetheless, I learned a lot about myself and what

I needed to adjust to be more successful at work. It helped me take the right actions.

The thing to remember about strengths is that we don't all have the same ones, and that's a good thing. When you commit to valuing the diverse strengths of others, that's when things can really be fruitful at work. Think about it: you might have a penchant for what people call "soft skills," like empathy and communication, and others might have more technical skills, like spreadsheet expertise or software development. We need all of those things for a well-functioning workplace. Can you think of a time when you worked really well with someone who had different but complementary skills? It was magic, right?

One of the last things I want to mention here is that it is crucial to document your strengths and accomplishments so that you can mention them in interviews, in project meetings, and subtly when interacting with those you want to influence. This might sound interesting to you, but what it is really is you using what you have to get exactly what you want when *you* want it. My son, who is now a senior in high school, is my only child who has set his sights high on military academies and Ivy League schools. We knew going into this journey that it would require him to have a calendar filled with advanced classes, sports, and extracurricular activities. Instead of a traditional journal or list, I used an app on my iPhone that allowed us to create a visualization of all of the required categories and then an inventory of his activities that fit within those categories. While it is a lot, it makes it significantly easier to pull up that one-page visualized representation of his accomplishments when completing applications. I think this is a great idea for anyone to use if they have their eyes set on achieving a certain goal. You could give this a try and see if it works for you too.

Now that you know more about identifying your strengths, let's delve into ways for you to develop them too.

Developing Your Strengths

If you believe in having the mindset that you can change, grow, and get better, then it is equally important to develop the strengths that you have and those that might not be apparent to everyone around you. There are three areas to focus on to develop what's already inside of you, described next.

- Focused improvement: This journey to self-leadership is not one of perfection, as we discussed earlier in the book; it is one of continuous small improvements. How?
  - Practice often. I know that one of my strengths is public speaking, and I also know that I shine in that strength when I put in the time to practice and then practice some more. Then my nerves are put to rest and I get to focus on my audience. You can do this, no matter your job function.
  - Learn continuously. Are you a student of life? Are you someone with a big appetite for learning new things? This is who you want to be if you want to develop your strengths. I have a friend I have written about many times who reads 100 books per year. He is in a constant search for new ideas, ways to improve his thinking and his behaviors. He doesn't see his learning coming with a deadline, but from a fountain that never runs out. Do you embrace this philosophy? I am learning from him and getting better at this.
  - Challenge yourself. Have you ever thought about taking on projects that are a little outside of your comfort zone, or even not in an area in which you normally work? Has someone presented an opportunity to you, but you declined for fear of not knowing anything about the project? I want to challenge you to think outside your standard way of being and take more risks that move you

out of your comfort zone and stretch you to reveal and develop more strengths. If you want to be considered for certain roles or projects, you have to show up differently and more confidently than you have in the past. When you do, you will grow in your belief in yourself, and others around you will too.

- Leveraging strengths in teams: In the next chapter, I will hyper-focus on relationship-building as a way to demonstrate self-leadership and be a more successful professional at work. For now, I want to mention that you can learn to contribute your strengths within your team to benefit the team, despite what title you hold. When you adopt this type of team focus, you can have a huge impact on your team's performance. You will also stand out, since often people at work focus on getting ahead or looking out for themselves. When your colleagues see you are interested in advancing team goals, they will see and treat you differently. You get to choose to be this type of teammate. No need for permission.

- Mentorship and coaching: I have already mentioned a few times how critical it is for you to seek out mentors or engage a coach. It is equally important to do so if you want to develop your strengths in a more intentional way. I have coached many executive-level leaders who were already at the top of their game, but they knew that they needed to continue to understand their blind spots and their areas of brilliance. Early on in my career, I hired a leadership coach. As an entrepreneur, I have also had business coaches to help me dig up what was in front of me, but I couldn't see things by myself. Find a way to find these resources and lean on them and trust them to give you a different perspective.

Now that I have shed some light on how to develop your strengths, let's take a closer look at how to consistently apply those strengths.

Applying Your Strengths

I try not to be theoretical in my writing, but I know that I can sometimes lean in that direction. This section is where the rubber meets the road and where your application of the strengths that you have uncovered and developed comes to life. When you proactively apply what you learn about what's inside of you, your brilliance becomes much like that Golden Buddha in the introduction, shining for others to see. Here are three distinct ways that applying your newly highlighted strengths can improve your workplace experience and even advance you in your career path:

- Improved decision-making: One of the less obvious but significantly important benefits of playing to your strengths is how doing so can improve your decision-making. Think about it – if you are taking on new roles and projects that make you shine, or that feel the most natural for you, you will more naturally be able to move those things forward. This forward movement will highlight for those around you how your thinking improved in those new roles. You will also become more confident in your decisions when you put yourself in those positions and succeed. I remember working for one leader who seemed to doubt that I could work with clients in an objective way and still maintain strong relationships. I think she saw me as "soft" in my approach, giving in too much to client requests. On one client visit, I decided to ask her to join me. She saw that I was very effective in meeting clients where they were, listening closely but never overpromising, and also reflecting our company's main initiatives and values in the process. I walked away from that scenario even more confident in my role, and she was very impressed with my style and finesse with the client. I was definitely in the right role for me and the company.

- Creating opportunities: One of the ways to play to your strengths is to propose new projects or initiatives that move your organization forward and help your team shine. Applying your strengths often creates opportunities for synergy, where the combined efforts of multiple individuals produce a result greater than the sum of their separate effects. For example, if you are a strong organizer and project manager, you can bring together a team with diverse skills, ensuring that each member's strengths are utilized effectively. This coordination leads to successful project outcomes and reinforces the value of the alliance.

- Create a positive work environment: When you apply your strengths, you contribute to a positive and productive work environment. This positivity can be contagious, encouraging others to also focus on their strengths and seek out alliances that enhance their abilities. A positive environment nurtures collaboration and innovation, making it easier to form and maintain strong work alliances. Demonstrating your strengths consistently helps build your credibility and trust within the workplace. When others see you delivering high-quality work reliably, they are more likely to seek your input and consider you a valuable ally. This trust forms the foundation for strong work alliances. For example, if you are known for your problem-solving abilities, team members will turn to you for guidance during complex projects, fostering a collaborative environment.

Consider a sports team where each player excels in a specific position. The star striker's ability to score goals is complemented by the midfielder's skill in creating opportunities and the defender's prowess in protecting the goal. When each player focuses on their strengths, the team as a whole becomes more cohesive and effective, forming a powerful alliance that drives success. Now you're in the driver's seat to find your perfect role that highlights your strengths all around you.

Bright Ideas for Self-Leadership

Reflective Writing: Discovering Your Strengths

Write a reflective essay on your own strengths. Identify at least three strengths you demonstrated in these situations. Use examples from personal, academic, or work contexts. This will help you develop self-awareness about your strengths and how they manifest in various situations.

Assessment Comparison and Analysis

Take at least two of the DiSC, CliftonStrengths, and Myers-Briggs assessments.

Complete each assessment and analyze the results. Compare the similarities and differences in the results from each assessment. Reflect on how these assessments align with your own perceptions of your strengths.

360-Degree Feedback Simulation

Conduct a simplified 360-degree feedback with peers, colleagues, or classmates. Select a few people who know you well in different contexts (e.g. work, school, social). Ask them to provide feedback on your strengths and areas for improvement. Summarize the feedback in a report. This will help you gain insight into how others perceive your strengths and areas for development.

Strengths Inventory and Visualization

Create a visual representation of your strengths and accomplishments. Use a tool like an app or a digital platform to document your strengths, skills, and significant achievements. Organize them into categories and create a visual dashboard.

Social Interaction and Influence

This final part of the book centers on the part of self-leadership that is more outward focused. It's where the inner work begins to connect to the external world and rely more on it for our personal and professional success. In it, I will delve into the importance of relationships, flexible thinking and being, setting clear expectations, giving and receiving feedback, and more effectively using our voices with others.

8

Relationship-Building in Action

This chapter is focused on relationship-building, which is what helps us cross over from leading ourselves for our own sake to having more influence on others.

You may wonder why I put the chapter on relationships at this point in the book, or maybe why I am including this chapter at all. Look back at my definition of self-leadership, a part of which is "the journey of growing inwardly to shine outwardly." I want to address that outward shine a bit. It is next to impossible not to be in a relationship with others. How we lead ourselves directly impacts those relationships. I do want to be clear, though, that it is quite critical for you to focus on self-leadership first and then leadership for others. Remember, the inward growth is what should be at the top of your list. Let me reiterate something I referred to in Chapter 1: you are perfectly imperfect. You are more than good. This idea of growing inwardly has more to do with revealing the shine that is already in you. Just like that Golden Buddha was worth a fortune no matter the clay that covered it, you are worth more than you know, and this book is meant to help you embody your greatness, displaying it for the world to see.

This chapter will focus primarily on establishing trust, effective communication, collaborative teamwork, and network building, all with an eye on building strong relationships that benefit you personally and professionally. You will connect all that you have learned and use it to curate a personal and workplace experience that puts you back in control of your life, no longer waiting for permission or "green lights." First, let's focus on the ways that building trust opens the doors of possibilities for you and enables you to display your shine outwardly.

The Foundation of Trust

Imagine trust in the workplace as an invisible glue that holds the intricate structure of an organization together. It's not always seen, but its absence is immediately felt. Trust is a dynamic force, evolving through consistent actions and open communication. Trust in the workplace can be defined as the firm belief in the reliability, truth, ability, or strength of someone or something within the professional environment. It's the assurance that your colleagues will act in your best interests, uphold their commitments, and maintain transparency.

I love how my friend Stephen M.R. Covey talked about trust in his acclaimed book *The SPEED of Trust: The One Thing That Changes Everything*: "In a high-trust relationship, you can say the wrong thing, and people will still get your meaning. In a low-trust relationship, you can be very measured, even precise, and they'll still misinterpret you." Without strong trust, there is no possible way to build strong bridges between people. If we don't have trust, our attempts at communicating, collaborating, or networking will be in vain.

"Compared with people at low-trust companies, people at high-trust companies report: 74% less stress, 106% more energy at work, 50% higher productivity, 13% fewer sick days, 76% more engagement, 29% more satisfaction with their lives, 40% less burnout" (Zak 2017).

I would go further to say that when I have worked in companies where I trust my manager, colleagues, senior leadership, and coworkers, I felt excited to get up and out of bed and do great work every day. I didn't dread work or my relationships there.

Although I will address more about collaboration a little later in this chapter, it's important to note here that trust is the bedrock of collaboration. When team members trust each other, they are more willing to share ideas, take risks, and collaborate effectively. This trust reduces the fear of criticism and failure, enabling innovative thinking and problem-solving. Think about it: in a high-trust environment, an employee is more likely to propose a novel idea during a brainstorming session, confident that their contribution will be valued rather than ridiculed. Do you find this to be true for you too?

Trust also minimizes misunderstandings and conflicts. When trust is present, team members give each other the benefit of the doubt and resolve disputes amicably. In a high-trust environment, a disagreement over project details is approached with a focus on finding common ground rather than assigning blame.

So how can you learn to build trust with those in your personal and professional life?

- Consistency and reliability: You build trust through consistent actions. Keeping promises, meeting deadlines, and maintaining reliability are essential for establishing trust.

Have you ever worked with someone or even someone in your family who talked a good game, but when the time came to *do* something, they always fell short? You probably had very little trust in them. If people cannot rely on you, they won't trust you, which means they won't offer opportunities to you or introduce you to people who could open doors for you.

- Transparency and openness: You will build trust when you are open about your decisions, share information freely, and explain your rationale behind actions. Can you think of a person in your life who always seemed to be telling "half-truths" or not the whole story and left you wondering what they were leaving out? I once worked with someone like that. He would make rounds in the office, trying to grab any information he could from everyone else, but never quite disclosed what he was up to with the requests. It felt slimy talking to him in those moments too.

- Empathy and compassion: I promise, when you show empathy and compassion to colleagues and those around you in your personal life, you show them that you care, and you build emotional bonds with them. In this very divided and self-centered world, you differentiate yourself by choosing to show up this way for others. Just like I wrote about you filling your own self up so that you can do the same for others, this is the place where self-leadership growth reveals itself to those around you and this is where the good stuff of life and work combine to make real relationships that last a lifetime.

- Accountability and integrity: When we are accountable to ourselves and live in integrity with what we say we stand for, we build trust with others in powerful ways. It rubs me the wrong way when others don't take responsibility for their actions or admit their own mistakes. This is the crux of self-leadership and critical for maintaining trust. Honestly, I catch myself occasionally showing up with victim thinking, but then I see the thing in myself that drives me nuts, and I stop myself from going too far. I remind myself that I am the person in charge of my choices, and thus I am also responsible for much of my results. It can be a tough thing to look at ourselves in the mirror and be honest. No matter, to be good leaders of self, we must do it often. If we want others to trust us, we will make this a habit.

- Recognition and appreciation: We all want to be valued for our contributions at home, at work, and in our communities. This helps to validate our purpose and ties closely to the theme of Chapter 1, "Understanding Your Intrinsic Worth." If you want to be trusted by those around you, genuinely recognize and appreciate their contributions to the team. This is not just something for managers to do either. No matter your role, you should focus on providing authentic recognition to your coworkers as a way to build trust. Gallup found:

Among employees with great recognition experiences, 72% say that performance for little things is commonly recognized at their organization, compared with 16% of employees with poor recognition — defined as the worst recognition experience across all five pillars.
—Stevens and Kemp 2023

It is worth restating that if you want to build and maintain trust, which is at the core of true relationship-building, focus on finding the small things that your coworkers and even your family do and show sincere appreciation to them for those things. It is just the special touch that will make them think of and remember you fondly.

As a side note, you might be wondering how to repair trust when it is broken, given how important it is for relationship success. As someone who has already come this far to focus in on the inner part of self-leadership, you now know that admitting mistakes is a huge trust builder. It is also a big trust "rebuilder" too. There is nothing more disarming than *not* placing blame on someone else for something you did wrong. You will immediately endear people to you when you don't place blame elsewhere. The vulnerability that it takes on your part not to *act* perfect in a situation where things go wrong immediately softens hearts, calms conflicts, and dispels any doubt that you can be trusted.

Next, we will dig deep into the role that effective communication plays in building bridges between you and those you seek to influence in some way.

Effective Communication

The area of communication is a big one. It's a two-way street that determines a significant amount of our success, both personally and professionally. The problem with many of us is that we focus on hearing our own voices and interacting in ways that we most understand. If we are to let our brilliance shine through, we must learn the skills and strategies to communicate in ways that are clearer and meet others where they are to receive the messages we have to provide them.

There are three communication skills that I believe are the key differentiators: being clear in your messaging, learning to actively listen, and understanding and responding to different communication styles. We need to do all of this inside the backdrop of a digital-first world. When you think about the times when others were confused by an email you sent, or even someone's body language in a virtual meeting, communication effectiveness might be the biggest challenge we face now and into the future.

Clearer Communication

Do you think you are a clear communicator? Have you ever surveyed friends, family, or coworkers on this? I thought I was very clear in my communication, especially when it came to my personal brand, but then I was courageous enough to ask two professionals I trust to audit the clarity of my brand. A few months later they were ready to share their results. One told me that he loved what I stood for, but that I needed to choose a lane that was crystal clear for those in my audience. I thought I was clear, but if he was confused, then I needed to get to work in making it clearer. What have you done to ensure you are clear in your own communications?

In 2023, I felt this topic was so important that I partnered with LinkedIn Learning to create a course on "Communicating with Clarity for Managers." I outlined the missteps and some ways to bypass being seen as vague and ineffective, like being specific, using examples and analogies, proofreading, and more (Younger 2023a). No matter your position, you can learn to be a clear communicator and increase your influence and connections with others to achieve more and be more. When you think about all the hard work you do every day to develop that inner shine, communicating clearly allows that brilliance to shine through.

Clear communication ensures that your message is easily understood, while brevity respects the time and attention of your audience. Here are a few tips to help you on your way to becoming a clearer communicator:

- Simplify your message: Use straightforward language and avoid jargon or overly complex terms. The whole point of becoming a more effective communicator is to connect with people and use your words to build stronger relationships. If you always use acronyms and abbreviated sayings, you may potentially create more of a disconnect with those around you.

- Be direct: Get to the point quickly and avoid unnecessary details. This is especially true when you are dealing with certain communications styles (more on this below). Even when you're telling a story, share only the most important details of that story so others can understand the experience.

- Use visual aids: If you are doing some type of presentation, supplement your words with visuals like charts, diagrams, or slides to enhance understanding, but choose carefully. When I first started to do presentations, I tended to use 45 slides with many words on them, which was not effective. Now during my keynotes, the majority of my slides show either images only or just a word or two.

Clarity and brevity help prevent misunderstandings and ensure that your audience retains your key points. This approach also enhances your credibility and makes your communication more persuasive. This all culminates in more influential communication too.

One area that is overlooked as an important aspect of communication is active listening, so next we'll explore the elements of great active listening.

Active Listening

Communication goes both ways and that means that a speaker expresses ideas, wants, and concerns and then there *should* be a listener on the other end trying to gather up what the speaker is saying. Many of us drop the ball on effective listening and leave people around us feeling unseen and unheard. I have spent a great portion of my work life honing the skill of active listening, because I have found through my research that a person's worth and their success with building long-term relationships centers on truly learning how to listen actively. I believe in this so much that I wrote a book on this topic, created a certification around it, and even created another LinkedIn Learning course on the subject, titled "Active Listening for Better Leadership Communication" (Younger 2023b). Although that was meant to be a primer on the much more in-depth work I do on this topic, I wanted to share my proprietary framework, called "The Cycle of Active Listening™," with people around the globe. Whether you lead yourself and your family but don't manage anyone at work or you lead a large team or enterprise, everyone can benefit from learning a more effective way to listen to those who expect us to hear them. When you reflect on what self-leadership means, active listening is the doorway to remove the clay that covers many of our relationships to reveal the good from within.

Here is an overview of my process for active listening that I sincerely hope you will adopt, in practice, in your very next interaction:

1. Recognize the unsaid. This is when you slow down long enough to notice what signals people are giving you about their wants and needs, but for some reason they are not speaking up about them. Once you realize that people aren't speaking up, your curiosity increases, and then you move on to seek to understand.

2. Seek to understand. This is when you lean in to uncover what the unspoken words might mean, and act in a way that invites others to share their truth openly with you. Your focus here is serving them with your full and complete presence.

Also, commit to minimizing assumptions and ridding yourself of biases that make you presuppose what someone needs from you. It will serve you much better to lean in to find the other person's truth than replace their truth with your truth.

3. Decode the message. This step is when you break down all that you learn in the seeking step to think about what it means and what you and those on your team will do about it. You might research it, or work with other colleagues to evaluate the feedback. When you take the time in this step, you make the person providing the feedback feel more important than they previously thought.

4. Take action. This step is where the rubber meets the road in active listening. This is where people can see the direct connection between their feedback and your level of compassion.

5. Close the loop. This is the step when you make sure to go back to the person who gave you feedback or expressed a concern and let them know what you will do about it, or that you found a compromise, or that you will be unable to do anything about it. When you do this, you show them respect and deepen their trust in you.

Now that you have a better understanding of the impact and need to actively listen as a way of building relationships and understanding the intent of other people, let's look more closely at communication styles.

Understanding Communication Styles

As I mentioned in Chapter 7, I like to use DiSC® communication styles to help others understand how their style and communication preferences affect their success in their relationships with others. While I do up to a full day of training on this as a certified DiSC trainer, I am going to provide an overview of the four distinct communication styles here, because they are the easiest to understand and use in your everyday interactions (see Figure 8.1). I also believe that they are the window into the needs of others and how to meet them where they are to achieve more in our own leadership journey.

Four styles make up the DiSC acronym. The D communication style represents a person who is dominant in their decision-making, moves fast in many areas of their life, and focuses more on task achievement with an eye to achieving some level of success. You will recognize the D because they usually talk fast, walk fast, and make decisions fast. They are most often focused on achieving lofty goals, because they feel most alive when they are crushing goals.

The I communication style is someone who is influential, because they focus on people and what is happening to and with them. They are most alive when they are with people and having fun with them. They move fast like the D, but their main focus is on people and not tasks. You can spot a high I if they are super excitable when talking to people, and they are often the life of the party. When things get boring, someone with the I style engages with and brings life to what is happening around them.

	Pace	Priority
D	Quick	Task
I	Quick	People
S	Deliberate	People
C	Deliberate	Task

FIGURE 8.1 DiSC® communication style matrix.

The S communication style is known to be steady and more deliberate in everything they do. The S is much more focused on people than they are on tasks, but even with tasks they need to understand the process and even create a process to help them and others move forward. You can spot the S because they are thinking through how a new change might impact someone on the team or some other person and making sure the change is methodical.

The C communication style is very conscientious. They are like the D in that their focus is on task completion, but they are more deliberate in their actions like the S and really need data and procedures to help them make decisions and execute on tasks. You will know you or someone else is a C when they are frustrated because things are moving so quickly before they've done any research or understand the numbers and impacts behind the change. The C will make sure everything is just so and will triple-check the accuracy of things.

The easiest way to determine your own default communication style is to ask yourself these two questions: (1) What is my speed? (2) What is my focus or priority? When you answer these questions, you will be clearer about your main default style based upon the table in Figure 8.1. Keep in mind that many people have two or three styles, so a little of each style will show up in one person, but more often than not the default style shows up first.

While I am just touching the surface of what makes up each of these styles and preferences, I think it's important to talk a little about the impact of these styles on one another, particularly at work. While understanding your own style is important, the key is figuring out how to influence others by using the intersection of your communication preference and the preferences of others with whom you work. For example, if your manager is a high D and you are a high S, you might encounter some friction when you ask for more justification or even explanation on a change taking place, because the high D is most interested in achieving a successful outcome in the quickest amount of time, instead of needing to understand how every aspect of the change impacts every person in the process. For the S to be successful in working with that D, the S needs to focus on keeping things short and sweet and making sure that the D is aware of how the path that the S proposes will help the D win and is faster than the original plan. The S will frustrate the D if the S moves slowly or spends too much time on details and impacts to people.

On the other end of the spectrum, if you are a high I and you are working with a high C, from a communication preference perspective you are dealing with opposites as well. Remember, the I likes to move fast and the C is much more deliberate. The I wants to interact and talk and have fun with people and the C is looking to complete their tasks on time, but with great accuracy and deliberation, and the impacts to people are not their main concern. You can see how, without the right awareness and strategies to meet both parties closer to their preference, conflicts will arise.

If any of these parties seek to grow in influence, they must learn to adapt to the communication styles and preferences of others around them. One of the most critical things to learn as someone who seeks to influence an audience, a decision, or a situation is how to read the room and adjust your communication style. Sometimes, without even knowing it, we might enter into a tense situation and then expect others to change their energy or how they are feeling and communicate with us the way we want them to. While this would be wonderful, it is more critical to learn how to lead yourself in that situation and come to the middle with what is taking place in that moment. For example, if you are someone who tends to be happy all the time and high energy – most likely an I – then entering a room where everyone seems heated or deep in thought means you will need to come down a bit in energy. I don't mean that you need to become heated too, but coming closer to the energy in the room will send the signal to those in that room that you can adjust for the situation. By doing so, you grow in influence, because they can see that you have high social awareness.

I mentioned earlier the importance of active listening in keying into the unspoken cues in our environment. Another thing to highlight here is the need to be empathetic to what might be happening at any given time, which is closely tied to paying attention to unspoken and spoken signals. Empathy is sensing the need of another person and really leaning in to understand those needs. If we want to be known as a great communicator, we need to be equally great at being empathetic. I don't mean fake empathy; I mean genuinely caring about the needs of another. This means that we need to adjust how we show up to be fully present to understand that other person's experience. If we are too concerned with how "we" feel and what "we" will get out of the interactions or situations we are in, adapting to their style will not be possible. People want to follow and be around those who understand them and lean in to be present with them. By growing in empathy, you automatically influence how people see you and themselves.

People want to follow and be around those who understand them and lean in to be present with them.

Following are some other practical ways that you can grow in influence by understanding different communication preferences and adapting your style to grow in influence as well:

- Adaptive communication: Just because you uncovered that you have one default communication style does not mean that you can't use what you know about the four different styles to persuade and influence decisions and behaviors at work or at home. And before you jump to thinking this is manipulative, I want to share an example to illustrate that meeting people where they are to achieve more, together, is not a bad thing at all.

Many years ago, I was working in a tech start-up in a sales/account management role. As a mid-level manager responsible for bottom-line results, I knew that the executive leadership team most appreciated very detailed and data-focused sales presentations. Admittedly, I am a high I and have very little C in me. So numbers and details are not my strength, but I knew an analyst in sales enablement who was amazing at that. Instead of going to him with a whining story and too much fluff, I went to him and stated the problem, gave him the exact three things I needed from him, and explained the way that I would prefer the data presented. What he gave me a few days later was exactly what I needed! I knew that he was more of a C and an S than he was an I or a D. So I met him where he was to make him feel seen by my adapting my style to his and also getting what I needed in return. The sales presentation turned out beautifully and the executive team was thrilled. Of course, I gave my sales enablement colleague some of the credit, and my relationship with him is still going strong today and we work together as consultant colleagues often.

- Sincere recognition: If you want to influence people anywhere on the planet, show them sincere appreciation and recognition. Think about it. What would you do for the people who have stepped up and shown you authentic appreciation at work? Almost anything, right? Be very liberal in your appreciation. I remember seeing a TINYpulse survey some years ago that said that people at work will leave their job for one that shows them consistent recognition. Gallup also shared research that people at work don't even remember being recognized unless it was in the last seven days. This means that getting good at expressing our appreciation for others can change their world and ours.

In a former job, I remember some of my colleagues questioning how I had so much time to recognize people in the office. I told them that I make it a priority, because I know that none of us get recognized enough for the work we put in, big or small. Personally, partly because I am a high I, and partly because of the dopamine boost I get when I get recognition, I *love* giving recognition too. I have had people mention how they always feel important and valued around me. My actions endeared them to me for a long time. That is influence in action! While not everyone likes to be recognized in the same way, go out of your way to find out how your colleagues prefer to be shown appreciation and do that often!

Now that we understand the importance of clear communication, the role of active listening, and the knowing and adapting to communication styles to leverage our own self-leadership potential, let's look at the role of collaborative teamwork.

Collaborative Teamwork

An African proverb says, "If you want to go fast, go alone. If you want to go far, go together." It speaks to the importance of cooperation for long-term success. While working with others can be challenging for those who prefer to work quickly, the proverb suggests that collaboration is essential for making real progress. Consider all the times you were faced with a big, scary goal or a company initiative and you wondered how the heck you could achieve it alone. Then you started to bring more people into the discussion and realized that the goal was attainable, because you weren't alone at all. This is the power of teamwork, and it cannot be understated in the context of self-leadership.

One of the things that we also need to remember is that we must bring new and different people around our decision-making table. I say this whether you manage a home, a team, or an entire organization. Make sure you are intentional about including people from different departments and different backgrounds so that you can leverage different perspectives to come up with more innovative solutions to your challenges. If you stick with the same people and their thinking, you will get the same outcomes you've been getting.

I have personally experienced this when working with a coach. After a while, I needed to shift which coach I worked with to continue to learn and grow and think differently, and thus get new and better outcomes.

> *If you stick with the same people and their thinking, you will get the same outcomes you've been getting.*

I wrote earlier about the need to adopt a genuine recognition environment that uplifts people in specific and intentional ways. In the context of collaborative teamwork and making sure that everyone is bought into the mission and the success of the team, celebrating team success and achievements builds strong bridges between the members of the team. When each of the team members is excited and inspired to win for the team and not for the individuals, they can achieve wonderful things. This kind of thinking puts you in a much better place to experience the kind of group performance that can transform organizations.

Just recently, my son, Dominic, attended Boys' State, which is a camp for rising high school seniors sponsored by the American Legion to teach them about civics and Americanism. We discovered this program after watching a documentary about it on a streaming service a couple of years ago. So Dominic was aware of the process and even had his eye on which elected position he wanted before even registering. When Dominic arrived at the camp and jumped into city formation and the election process with all the speech-making, he observed that many young men really pushed to communicate their platform and the position for which they wanted to run. Dominic wanted to join in, but felt strange about focusing on himself so much. Instead, he decided to focus on working with the other young men to build the best city that they could. He noticed where his campmates could really use their skills to lead well in certain positions, he focused on helping them win their seats, he listened more than he spoke, and he cheered everyone on from the sidelines. While he did do some campaigning too, most of his focus was on the needs and pains of his campmates. In the end, he was asked to run for the position that he wanted, because he became the natural candidate for the position. His focus on celebrating and elevating those around him expanded his influence, helped create the best city, and he made amazing friends in the process too. We can all learn to celebrate those around us and combine our shine with theirs to create amazing results.

Before I move on from the topic of teamwork, I want to address one toxic behavior that will never serve you or your team members well, and that is gossip. This is an awful thing that people do usually when they are insecure in their own position or accomplishments or a lack thereof. When someone says something to you about another behind the other's back, stand in your shoes and don't respond in agreement or judgment. Rather, tell the gossiper that neither of you have the facts to be able to talk about or judge the other person, and then end the conversation. Alternatively, you can challenge the gossiper's thinking to have them think in a more positive way about the persona about whom they are gossiping. It's very easy to go along to get along, but as you focus on leading yourself much better, pause your inclination to insert your opinion, which is often not grounded in facts. By taking this pause and this more neutral position, you preserve the power of the team.

Now that you know more about the value in collaborative teamwork, let's go deeper to see how you can advance your career through networking and mentorship.

Networking and Mentorship

It's been said that you are the company you keep, meaning with whom you choose to spend your time greatly determines your mindset and your direction.

In today's interconnected world, building a strong network beyond your immediate team is crucial for personal and professional growth. Expanding your network within the broader organization and industry can open doors to new opportunities, foster innovation, and provide valuable support systems. Here's a guide to help you navigate this process effectively.

Recognize the Importance of a Broader Network

Honestly, for the majority of my life, I haven't called upon others to advance in my career. As an only child, I really have been a self-reliant person. As I became a more seasoned professional, I could see how much networking and stepping outside of what I could do on my own would get me further than doing it all alone. I could also build relationships with like-minded people. Expanding your network beyond your immediate teammates is essential for a few other reasons:

- Career advancement: A broad network can provide insights into potential career opportunities, mentorship, and support from influential professionals. Why limit yourself? Step outside your comfort zone to go as far as you can.

- Resource sharing: Collaboration with a wider group of individuals increases the likelihood of accessing valuable resources and expertise that can aid in achieving your goals. While the broader network is a good thing, make sure you start within your organizations first. Begin by building connections within your current organization. Here are some strategies to help you make the most of what's right in front of you:

  - Attend cross-departmental meetings: Participate in meetings and projects that involve multiple departments. This allows you to meet colleagues from different areas of the organization and understand their roles and challenges. It also gets more eyes on the work you are doing and the skills and gifts you bring to the table. I remember doing this while working as a mid-level manager at a blood center. I would attend technical and medical groups whose work touched on my work in the way I and my team served clients. I could be there to listen and learn, but also make myself be known and establish relationships.

  - Join employee resource groups (ERGs): ERGs are a great way to connect with colleagues who share similar interests or backgrounds. These groups often provide networking events, professional development opportunities, and a platform to share ideas. Even if you are not a part of one of the groups represented, they often want allies to join their meetings and help advance their efforts. You are welcome in most cases.

  - Leverage internal social platforms: Use company intranets, internal social networks, or collaboration tools like Slack or Microsoft Teams to engage with colleagues. Participate in discussions, share insights, and contribute to ongoing projects. If you are going to be spending 40-plus hours per week at your job, you might as well get the most of it.

Cultivate Relationships in Your Network

Building a network is not just about making connections; it's about nurturing them. Admittedly, I did not nurture my relationships enough until just recently when I realized how good it felt to have others on this journey with me and to be on their journey with them. Here are some tips that I use today:

- Follow up: After meeting someone new, follow up with a personalized message or email. Mention something specific from your conversation to remind them of who you are and express your interest in staying in touch.

- Offer value: Networking is a two-way street. Offer your help, share resources, or provide introductions to others. Being generous with your time and expertise builds trust and reciprocity.

- Stay consistent: Regularly check in with your contacts. Share updates about your work, congratulate them on their achievements, and arrange occasional meetups or virtual coffee chats.

Expanding your network beyond immediate teammates requires intentional effort and strategic actions. By leveraging opportunities within your organization, engaging with industry peers, and cultivating meaningful relationships, you can build a robust network that supports your career growth and professional success. Remember, networking is not just about what you can gain but also about how you can contribute to the growth and success of others. Finding a mentor and being one too can also completely change your personal and professional trajectory.

The Benefits of Mentorship

Mentorship is a powerful tool for career development. A survey conducted by Sun Microsystems comparing 1,000 employees over a five-year period found that "Both mentors and mentees were approximately 20% more likely to get a raise than people who did not participate in the mentoring program" (Quast 2011). Engaging in mentorship can provide invaluable insights, guidance, and opportunities for your career advancement. Here's an exploration of the benefits of mentorship, both as a mentor and a mentee.

As a mentee, seeking out and building a relationship with a mentor has significant benefits:

- Guidance and support: A mentor provides advice based on their own experiences, helping you navigate career challenges and make informed decisions. Again, you don't have to do this life alone. It's much more enjoyable when you seek out and connect with people who care about you and your journey. I have formally and informally mentored people who showed me that they were focused on growth and were respectful of my time.

- Skill development: Mentors can offer practical knowledge and skills that are not always available through formal training. There is really nothing that can replace real-life examples lived by someone who is willing to impart their knowledge to you. Grab that when you have it available.

- Networking opportunities: I just shared the benefits of networking, and mentors often introduce mentees to their professional networks, opening doors to new opportunities and relationships. Why not step outside of that comfortable circle to engage with people you wouldn't ordinarily get to meet?

If you choose to be a mentor yourself, the benefits to you for being generous with your time are also vast. That same Sun Microsystems survey found, "Mentors are six times more likely to have been promoted to a bigger job" (Quast 2011). That is a great reason to sign up right away to be a mentor, and here are a few others:

- Leadership development: Mentoring hones leadership and coaching skills, which are valuable for career progression.

- Fresh perspectives: Interacting with mentees can provide new insights and ideas, keeping mentors updated on industry trends and innovative thinking. Your eyes might be open to new ways to overcome your own business challenges while you work with them.

- Personal fulfillment: Many mentors find great satisfaction in helping others succeed and in giving back to their professional community. I have always been open to mentoring, and it feels good to be able to contribute to someone else's success.

Even though the benefits of having a mentor have been studied and published wide and far, it can be scary to reach out to someone you see as more experienced or even senior to you. In fact, "76% of people think that mentors are important, but only 36% have one" (Comaford 2019).

I know that seeking out a mentor can be a little intimidating, especially if you are earlier in your career, but the benefits to you as a mentee are vast. Seek out mentorship in a proactive way, by looking for individuals whose careers you admire and who are willing to invest in your growth. Just start the relationship by asking for a small amount of time to pursue one thing that intrigues you about their career journey that might be similar to yours. Don't go straight to asking them to be your mentor until you build trust with them and they know you are committed to professional growth. When you build trust and demonstrate your value, they will then be intrigued by you. When you take it further and demonstrate your work ethic and drive to get certain results, they will most likely be thrilled to mentor you.

Mentorship is an invaluable component of career development. By engaging in these roles, both mentors and mentees can experience significant personal and professional growth. These relationships provide a pathway to knowledge, skill development, visibility, and career advancement, making them essential tools for anyone looking to succeed in their professional journey.

By embracing mentorship, you can unlock new levels of professional success and contribute to a culture of continuous growth and support within your organization and industry.

Nurturing and Sustaining Relationships

As you can tell, I think that building deep and sustaining relationships of trust is the key to growing in self-leadership. I can think of many ways in which not burning bridges but building them came full circle in my life and enhanced my professional journey. Can you?

Just recently, a meeting planner reached out to me after a long-term friend and former client recommended me to one of their events. I have known this friend, who started out as a client in a previous job, for over 15 years. She has been following my work ever since, and we would go on the occasional lunch catch-up too. When she was a client, I built a relationship of respect with her, always focusing on listening to her needs. As the years went by, one of us would reach out to touch base. This many years later and now I have a two engagements with the global organization for whom she works.

I have always been someone to reach out, by text or email, to people a few times per year to see how they are doing and to let them know that I am thinking about them. I started my relationship development efforts at the beginning of my career, and I have never let them go. Here are several ways for you to sustain long-term relationships that can serve you and others into the future:

- Even after you change roles or companies, keep in touch with those with whom you already had a strong relationship, by setting up coffee, lunch, virtual meetups, text messages, or networking event get-togethers.

- Mark your calendar with their birthdays or important dates in their lives and reach out to them. Send them a card. You will stand out and they will appreciate it.

- Even in a remote setting, prioritize touching base with colleagues and team members so they know you're thinking about them.

On your journey of self-leadership, you have moved from self-understanding to personal development and growth and have just journeyed through the rich road of relationship development. As you continue on your journey toward more effective social interactions and influence, remember that you choose how much clay remains over you and your connection to others. In the following chapter, we will be laser-focused on the importance of flexible thinking not only to expand your influence, but also to see the brighter side of life and work.

Bright Ideas for Self-Leadership

- **Reflect on trust:** Think about a time when trust played a crucial role in your interactions. Write a journal entry reflecting on how trust influenced the outcome. Consider how you can build or rebuild trust in current relationships.

- **Enhance communication skills:** Take a DiSC self-assessment to gauge your communication skills. Identify areas where you can improve, such as being more concise or listening actively. Practice these skills in your next interactions and note the changes.

- **Engage in networking:** Attend a cross-departmental meeting or an industry event. Make a goal to meet at least three new people. Follow up with them afterward to start building a professional relationship.

- **Mentorship search:** Identify someone you admire and respect in your field. Reach out to them for a mentorship opportunity. Additionally, consider how you can mentor someone else, providing guidance and support based on your experiences.

CHAPTER

9

Leaning into Flexible Thinking

In the late twentieth and early twenty-first centuries, Kodak was a leading company in photographic film. However, as digital photography began to emerge, Kodak clung to its traditional film business. Despite inventing the first digital camera in 1975, the company was reluctant to embrace this new technology for fear of cannibalizing its film business.

The problem was that Kodak's leadership was inflexible in their thinking, believing that their established business model and the dominance of film would continue to prevail. They underestimated the rapid advancement and consumer adoption of digital technology. Unfortunately, competitors like Sony and Canon embraced the digital photography and took over market share, which culminated in Kodak filing for bankruptcy. While Kodak has attempted to pivot and recover, it remains a cautionary tale of how inflexible thinking can lead to the downfall of even the most established companies.

In the simplest of terms, flexible thinking is when we are willing to change our thinking and our behaviors when different ideas arise or any kind of change is necessary. This kind of thinking is critical if we are to evolve, and to achieve what we set out to achieve, either alone or inside an organization. There are many benefits of this type of thinking, but I am going to address the most important in our current business climate:

- Improve problem-solving: Flexible thinkers are better equipped to handle complex and novel problems. They can devise multiple solutions and choose the most effective one. Because flexible thinkers also tend to be more resilient in handling stressful situations like abrupt change, they can regulate their emotions when problems arise.

- Adaptability: The ability to adjust thoughts and actions based on changing circumstances or feedback. This includes shifting strategies when current approaches are ineffective. As the above discussion demonstrates, this was an area Kodak really struggled to embrace.

- Creativity and innovation: The capacity to generate innovative ideas and approaches. Flexible thinkers often employ creative problem-solving techniques and think outside the box. When you don't confine your thinking to one outcome or set of outcomes or even one set of assumptions, you will find that you can think more flexibly about the possible solutions. This is when innovation takes shape.

For example, in the mid-2000s, Apple was primarily known for its successful line of personal computers and the iPod, a revolutionary music player. At that time, the smartphone market was dominated by companies like BlackBerry, Nokia, and

Motorola, which focused on physical keyboards and business-oriented features.

Steve Jobs, co-founder of Apple, demonstrated flexible thinking by envisioning a smartphone that combined the functionalities of an iPod, a phone, and an internet communicator. This vision led to the development of the iPhone, which deviated from the industry norms of the time.

Jobs challenged the conventional design of smartphones with physical keyboards and small screens. He envisioned a device with a large touch screen and a user-friendly interface. Instead of prioritizing business functions, Jobs emphasized an intuitive user experience that would appeal to a broad audience, from tech enthusiasts to everyday consumers. His innovations included things like the touchscreen interface that is so popular today, mobile internet browsing that made it easier to surf from our phones, and much more.

The iPhone quickly became a market leader, transforming Apple into one of the most valuable companies in the world. The iPhone sparked a wave of innovation in the smartphone industry, leading to the decline of companies that failed to adapt, like BlackBerry and Nokia (Cohan 2024). By embracing flexible thinking, Steve Jobs and his team at Apple were able to innovate and revolutionize the smartphone industry, setting new standards and redefining user expectations.

Whenever I uncover stories like this it inspires me to remain flexible in my thinking, but if I'm honest, I am not always flexible. I think I sometimes let problems of my past shape how I see challenges I face today, which can be problematic, because our world has changed and hardly anything is the same as it was many years ago. Breaking that thinking requires an openness to experience something different and set aside our fears for something revolutionary!

Now that we can see the benefits and importance of flexible thinking, let's look more closely at its foundations.

The Foundations of Flexible Thinking

One of the most important concepts to know and understand when thinking about flexibility is cognitive flexibility. Cognitive flexibility is "all about your brain's ability to adapt to new, changing, or unplanned events . . . and is also the ability to switch from one way of thinking to another" (Miller 2021). Think of it this way. Imagine your mind as a skilled gymnast on a balance beam. (See the case study about Simone Biles in Chapter 5.) Each task, challenge, or piece of new information is like a different routine the gymnast must perform. Cognitive flexibility is the ability of your mental gymnast to gracefully switch between routines, adapt to new movements, and maintain balance no matter the difficulty of the routine or the surprise elements introduced.

Just as a gymnast must switch between various routines (flips, turns, jumps) seamlessly, cognitive flexibility allows you to switch between different thoughts, ideas, or tasks smoothly, such as moving from analytical thinking when solving a math problem to creative thinking when brainstorming ideas for a project.

Looking more closely at my gymnast metaphor (Figure 9.1), cognitive flexibility also applies when unexpected elements are introduced during a performance, and a gymnast must quickly adapt their movements to maintain their balance and complete the routine successfully. Similarly, cognitive flexibility enables you to adapt your thinking and behavior when faced with new information or unexpected changes, ensuring you remain effective and balanced in your responses. Just as a gymnast adapts to the balance beam, an individual with cognitive flexibility can approach a problem from various angles, finding innovative solutions that a more rigid thinker might miss. It also allows you to understand and adapt to different viewpoints in a conversation, much like a gymnast adjusting their balance with every

FIGURE 9.1 Gymnasts as examples of cognitive flexibility.

move, leading to more harmonious and effective communication (Figure 9.2).

Embedded in this way of thinking is the mindset we choose to embrace. One of the most important things I learned on my journey is the idea of fixed mindset versus growth mindset. Renowned psychologist Carol Dweck is the person who introduced and labeled these different mindsets in her book *Mindset: The New Psychology of Success*, wherein she gives the science behind our mindsets and examples of how one type of mindset – the growth mindset – can serve us well, while having a "fixed mindset" rarely serves us. Dweck defines a fixed mindset as the belief that abilities, intelligence, and talents are innate traits that cannot be significantly developed. Individuals with a fixed mindset perceive their qualities as static and unchangeable, leading them to avoid challenges and give up easily in the face of obstacles (Dweck 2006, 6). Alternatively, Dweck writes about a better way to think about what she calls "growth mindset." Growth mindset is the belief that abilities and intelligence can be developed through dedication, effort, and learning. Individuals with

	Gymnast Skills	Cognitive Flexibility Skills	
	Balance Beam	**Precision and balance in decision-making**	
	– Precision	– Maintaining focus	
	– Balance	– Balancing different perspectives	
	Floor Exercise	Creative problem-solving and adaptability	
	– Creativity	– Generating innovative solutions	
	– Adaptability	– Adapting to new information	
	Vault	**Quick thinking and solution generation**	
	– Speed	– Rapid idea generation	
	– Power	– Quickly analyzing options	
	Parallel Bars	**Smooth transitions between tasks**	
	– Coordination	– Shifting smoothly between ideas/tasks	
	– Transitions	– Flexible thinking without losing focus	
	High Bar	**Confidence in intellectual risks**	
	– Strength	– Taking calculated intellectual risks	
	– Confidence	– Thinking outside the box	

FIGURE 9.2 Cognitive flexibility: becoming a mental gymnast.

a growth mindset see challenges as opportunities to improve and view failures as a natural part of the learning process (Dweck 2006, 7).

Every time I dive into these concepts, I realize that most of us move between both of these mindsets often, but some of us rely on one mindset more than others. While I admit that I can fall into a fixed mindset type of thinking here and there, I am more of a growth mindset person, because I might fall down or experience a setback, but then I jump back into figuring out what and how I can do better. My bounce-back might not be immediate, but in a very short time I can slap myself out of the fixed way of thinking. For example, as a professional speaker, I watch my attendees' event reviews very closely. I am cognizant of their comments, even when the positive feedback seems more moderate versus highly boisterous. I rarely get a critical comment, but when I do it's a little painful. I have to take a day or two to process it and then I snap myself out of it to focus on what I can control, which in this example is working on getting better based upon the feedback. This is because I know that I can and will get better with more practice and adjustments. This is the crux of the growth mindset.

Now that we know what flexible thinking can do for us, let's look at the flip side of cognitive flexibility and the growth mindset, which is cognitive rigidity, or that fixed mindset that Dweck wrote about extensively.

Cultivating a Growth Mindset

A fixed mindset is just another way to say that someone has cognitive rigidity, or rigid thinking, which makes them think that everything is either *this* or *that*, black or white, with no gray areas or the possibility to be or do something else. They believe that, if they aren't born with a particular talent, that can't be changed. Likewise, they think that if they didn't achieve something the first time, they never will. If you are to lead yourself from a place of strength and confidence, you cannot

A fixed mindset means that someone has rigid thinking, which makes them think that everything is either this or that, with no possibility to be or do something else.

hold on to a fixed mindset. In fact, I am telling you now: let it go! It does not and will not ever serve you and those you love and care for to have this mindset.

So what can you do to rid yourself of this way of thinking, or at least smack yourself out of it when you are stuck? Following are a few ways to overcome a fixed mindset.

Mindfulness and Awareness

Mindfulness – the practice of being present and fully engaged in the moment – is a powerful tool for enhancing self-awareness and promoting cognitive flexibility. By regularly engaging in mindfulness practices, you can develop a deeper understanding of your thought patterns, allowing you to identify and challenge rigid thinking.

Activities such as meditation, deep-breathing exercises, and mindful walking can help you become more attuned to your thoughts and feelings. These practices encourage you to observe your thoughts without judgment, providing a clearer perspective on how they influence your behavior and decision-making.

When you practice mindfulness, you become more aware of negative or limiting thoughts as they arise. This awareness creates an opportunity to interrupt these patterns and replace them with more positive, adaptive thinking. For example, if you notice a tendency to dismiss new ideas quickly, mindfulness can help you pause and consider them more openly.

Mindfulness fosters an open and nonjudgmental attitude toward experiences, which is essential for cognitive flexibility. By learning to accept and embrace the present moment, you become more adaptable and willing to explore new perspectives and possibilities.

Learning from Diverse Perspectives

Exposure to diverse perspectives and experiences is crucial for fostering flexible thinking. When you engage with people who have different backgrounds, cultures, and viewpoints, you expand your own understanding and challenge your assumptions.

Interacting with diverse individuals allows you to see the world from multiple angles. This can be achieved through traveling, reading books from different cultures, participating in multicultural events, or simply having conversations with people who have different life experiences.

Exposure to diverse perspectives helps you recognize and question your biases. For instance, a person who has only worked in one industry might have a limited view of what constitutes effective leadership. By learning about leadership styles in different fields, they can develop a more nuanced understanding.

To integrate diverse perspectives into your thinking, seek out opportunities to collaborate with colleagues from different departments or attend conferences in various industries. This will not only enhance your cognitive flexibility but also make you more innovative and adaptable.

Agree to Disagree: Understanding Without Agreeing

One of the critical aspects of flexible thinking is the ability to understand a perspective without necessarily agreeing with it. This approach, often summarized as "agree to disagree," promotes healthy dialogue and mutual respect.

When you engage in discussions with the goal of understanding rather than convincing, you open yourself to new ideas and reduce conflict. Approach conversations with curiosity, asking questions to gain clarity on the other person's viewpoint. This method allows for more productive and less confrontational interactions. By valuing understanding over agreement, you create an environment where diverse opinions can coexist, leading to more comprehensive and well-rounded decision-making.

For example, in a team meeting, if a colleague proposes a solution you initially disagree with, take the time to explore their reasoning. Ask questions like "Can you explain how this approach addresses our main challenges?" This can lead to a deeper understanding and possibly even a convergence of ideas that strengthens the final decision.

The Role of Curiosity

Curiosity is a fundamental driver of cognitive flexibility and lifelong learning. A curious mindset propels you to explore new ideas, ask questions, and seek out knowledge beyond your current understanding.

Cultivate a habit of asking "why" and "how" in your daily life. This practice encourages you to dig deeper into topics and understand the underlying principles behind them. Engage in activities that stimulate your curiosity, such as attending lectures, participating in workshops, or exploring new hobbies. Curiosity leads to continuous learning and growth. It motivates you to seek out new information, adapt to changing circumstances, and develop innovative solutions to problems. For example, a curious professional might explore emerging technologies in their field, leading to new insights and advancements.

Use curiosity to drive your self-leadership journey. When faced with a challenge, approach it with a curious mindset, asking questions like "What can I learn from this situation?" or "How can I approach this differently?" This attitude will help you remain open to new possibilities and adapt more effectively to change.

The Power of Reframing

In Chapter 4, I talked in detail about the need to learn how to use reframing as a way to bounce back from challenges or perceived failures. I believe in this tool so much that I want to mention it a couple times more. If you can learn to intentionally reframe what is happening in front of you or to you, your life will change. Yes, it is very human to have reservations, to occasionally get stuck in fixed thinking and ponder whether we have a way out of our current circumstance, but if you want to lead yourself better than you have in the past, reframing can make you think, "So that interview didn't go as well as I hoped. But at least I know I learned from it and can do better on the next one." Reframing is a tool that allows you to move right back into flexible thinking.

By integrating mindfulness practices, embracing diverse perspectives, practicing understanding without needing agreement, fostering curiosity, and owning your power to reframe, you can overcome cognitive rigidity and enhance your self-leadership. These strategies will not only promote flexible thinking but also empower you to navigate the complexities of personal and professional life with greater ease and resilience.

Implementing Flexible Thinking in the Workplace

Most of us work 40-plus hours per week. Work is the playground where we practice flexible thinking and test its effectiveness based upon the strength of our relationships and even our career trajectory. At work, flexible thinking is a must if we are to have flourishing cultures with constructive dialogue and to innovate together.

Work is the playground where we practice flexible thinking and test its effectiveness based upon the strength of our relationships and even our career trajectory.

Following are several practical ways to implement and benefit from flexible thinking, whether you manage a team or are a high-performing individual contributor.

Embrace Flexible Work Arrangements

If you are someone who leads a team and your organization will allow it, embrace flexible work hours or remote working options. This not only supports work-life balance but also encourages employees to think flexibly about how and where they work best. Your willingness might just deliver some unexpected levels of productivity and innovations. If you are an individual contributor, be open and flexible to new and different work arrangements too. When you show that openness, your managers, your team, and others in the organization will see you as a team player, which can be beneficial for your career.

Regular Feedback Loops

I will go into more depth about this in Chapter 11, but here I just want to say that you want to see feedback as a gift, whether you are giving it or receiving it. Take part in regular feedback loops where everyone can give and receive feedback. This continuous dialogue will help you adapt and improve processes and behaviors.

Problem-Solving Workshops

One of the things I do at the end of many of my keynotes, if I have enough time, is have attendees take part in a visualization exercise that takes them outside their normal thinking and calls on them to dream. I forbid them to use words like "no" and "can't" and "They won't approve that," because I know that it's easier not to own our own choices, journey, or outcomes, but it's worth it when we open the

I know that it's easier not to own our own choices, journey, or outcomes, but it's worth it when we open the space to do it.

space to do it. I love problem-solving workshops where employees work together to tackle real or hypothetical challenges. When we initiate or take part in these workshops or gatherings at work, it encourages brainstorming that allows for diverse and creative solutions. This is a wonderful way to promote flexible thinking.

One other thing to mention here is that we sometimes work in jobs that no longer meet our needs or we are limited in our career path. In these instances, people often think they need to stay at that job despite being unfulfilled. I want to impress upon you that life is too short to stay at a place that doesn't meet your goals and dreams. Instead, keep an open mind about new jobs in your current organization, taking on new projects that might meet your needs or even be open to moving to a new city or country to get what you need out of work. I was inspired by this truth when interviewing Jennifer Curtain on my *Leadership With Heart* podcast. Jennifer is the general manager at the Beatrice Hotel, a luxury boutique hotel in Providence, Rhode Island. When speaking to Jennifer, I could immediately feel her strong self-leadership. When I asked her about her leadership philosophy, Jennifer revealed that she leans in to flexible thinking and lives it every day. The snippet below was eye-opening and a wonderful example of open-mindedness as well;

> *It's about what you show up with everyday. I have not stopped, I am very motivated, whether it's new companies or new geographical locations, whatever it may be. Every time I felt like I needed a new challenge, I sought it out, and I used my mentors and the relationships that I made along the way to really make sure I was continuing to advance in my career . . . when I feel like I am reaching that plateau, I am ready for the next challenge.*
>
> —*Younger and Curtain 2024*

This sounds like a person who understands who she is, embraces her own development, seeks out and builds relationships with them, and then leverages mentors and colleagues to plot her own path. As such a strong self-leader, I knew I needed to include her voice in this book.

When we think about the state of our world with the emergence of AI technologies and rapid organization shifts via mergers and reorganizations, adapting a flexible way of thinking ensures our success and survival. It is thus worth it to practice this way of thinking in all aspects of our life.

Bright Ideas for Self-Leadership

- **Perspective-taking challenge:** Think of a recent disagreement or challenge you faced. Write a brief description of the situation from your perspective. Then write the same situation from the perspective of the other person involved. Reflect on the differences and similarities between the two perspectives. Consider what you can learn from this exercise and how it can help you in future interactions.

- **Diverse interaction diary:** For one week, make an effort to engage in conversations with people from different backgrounds or departments. Each day, note down at least one new perspective or idea you encountered. Reflect on how these new perspectives challenge or complement your existing views. At the end of the week, review your diary and identify any shifts in your thinking or new insights gained.

- **Curiosity exploration exercise:** Choose a topic you know little about but find interesting. Spend 30 minutes each day researching and learning about this topic for a week. Use a variety of sources such as articles, videos, podcasts, or books. At the end of the week, write a summary of what you've learned and reflect on how this new knowledge could be applied in your personal or professional life.

- **Flexibility in problem-solving:** Identify a current problem or challenge you're facing. List all the possible solutions you can think of, even the unconventional ones. For each solution, consider the potential outcomes and impacts. Discuss these solutions with a colleague, friend, or mentor to gain their input and perspective. Choose the most viable solution and implement it, remaining open to adjusting your approach based on feedback and results.

10

Expect Clear Expectations

Cristy's husband, Joe, started a new job with only two days of training. He is afraid to bother his manager by calling on him for clarity about what he can and cannot do in his new role, because his boss has 15 other things on his plate. Instead of sitting down with his new boss to establish priorities, Joe waits for his boss to reach out to him with objectives. In the meantime, Joe is unclear and frustrated, because he cannot move forward on projects that need to move forward soon.

Joe is experiencing what many people experience at work: a lack of clear expectations all around. In this chapter, I will drill down into the importance of clarity and how it fosters empowerment, performance, and job satisfaction. Remember, we are in Part III of this book, which focuses on the social interactions and influence we can wield if we

> *We need to empower ourselves and not wait to be empowered.*

follow the path in the first two parts. We spoke about empowerment in Chapter 6, which serves as a central theme of this book. We need to empower ourselves and not wait to be empowered.

Clear expectations are the foundation of effective self-leadership. They provide a sense of direction, ensure alignment, and foster accountability. By setting clear expectations for ourselves and others, we create an environment where goals are understood, efforts are coordinated, and success is achievable. When everyone is clear about what is expected of them, everyone benefits in some of the following ways:

- Clear expectations eliminate ambiguity, providing a precise understanding of what is required. This clarity enables individuals to focus their efforts on what truly matters, and not waste time on things that have minimal impact on what needs to get done.

- When expectations are clearly communicated, individuals feel more confident in their ability to meet them. This confidence boosts motivation and drives increased performance.

- Clear expectations promote open communication and mutual understanding, strengthening relationships and fostering a collaborative spirit. Everyone wins and feels like they're winning when things are clear.

Have you ever worked in an environment where you knew exactly what you needed to do and when? I've worked in both environments and the one with clear expectations was much more uplifting.

The Consequences of Poorly Set Expectations

In the realm of self-leadership, the ability to set and communicate clear expectations is paramount. Expectations guide our actions, influence our interactions with others, and shape the outcomes of our endeavors. When expectations are well defined and clearly communicated, they serve as a roadmap, leading us toward our goals with clarity and purpose. However, poorly set expectations can have significant negative consequences, creating confusion, frustration, and decreased productivity.

Confusion

When your expectations or the expectations of others are vague or ambiguous, it leads to confusion. Individuals are left unsure about what is required of them, resulting in wasted time and effort as they attempt to decipher the unclear directives. Without clear expectations, there is often a misalignment between what is expected and what is delivered. This misalignment can cause projects to veer off course, leading to unmet goals and disappointing outcomes.

A catastrophic example of how this can play out was when NASA launched the Mars Climate Orbiter, a robotic space probe intended to study the Martian climate, atmosphere, and surface changes. The mission was a collaboration between multiple teams, including NASA's Jet Propulsion Laboratory (JPL) and Lockheed Martin Astronautics. The project was complex, involving precise calculations and coordination among various teams (NASA Safety Center 2009).

One of the critical aspects of the mission was the navigation and control of the spacecraft. However, there was a significant misalignment in the expectations regarding the units of measurement used for navigation data:

- The engineering team at Lockheed Martin used English units (pound-seconds) for thrust calculations, while NASA's navigation team expected these calculations to be in metric units (newton-seconds).

- There was no clear protocol to verify and ensure that both teams were using the same units of measurement. This critical detail was overlooked due to the absence of explicit, unified expectations and communication.

The result of this misalignment was catastrophic. Due to the mismatch in units, the calculations for the spacecraft's trajectory were incorrect. The orbiter was set on a course that brought it too close to Mars. As the Mars Climate Orbiter approached Mars, it entered the planet's atmosphere at a much lower altitude than planned. The intense atmospheric friction caused the spacecraft to disintegrate, resulting in the loss of the $125 million mission. The primary objective of studying the Martian climate and atmosphere was left unachieved, and valuable scientific data that the mission was supposed to gather was never collected.

This incident underscored the critical importance of clear expectations and communication. The Mars Climate Orbiter mission serves as a stark reminder of how a lack of clear expectations and communication can lead to disastrous outcomes. In any project, especially those involving multiple teams and complex tasks, setting and verifying clear expectations are crucial to ensure alignment and achieve desired results. This real-world example illustrates the profound impact that clear expectations – or the lack thereof – can have on the success of a mission or project.

Often, the lack of clarity also leads to frustration on all sides.

Frustration

When expectations are not clearly communicated, individuals may unknowingly fall short of what is expected, leading to feelings of inadequacy and frustration. This can damage morale and reduce motivation. Poorly set expectations often result in misunderstandings and conflicts. When people are not on the same page, it creates friction and discord, disrupting harmony and collaboration within teams. I remember working with a cross-functional team on a large client's request. After leading a planning meeting, we thought we were clear about what we all individually needed to do to meet the client's needs until we made a big oversight on one of their deliveries. Our delay created a ripple effect for the client's supply chain, which made them doubt our ability to serve them. Everyone involved was frustrated by this mishap. Following this event, we put together a new process to ensure we didn't make the same mistake again. Sometimes, though, this lack of clarity can lead to a decrease in productivity too.

Decreased Productivity

Without clear expectations, individuals and teams may spend excessive time and resources on tasks that do not contribute to the desired outcome. This inefficiency hampers productivity and delays progress. For some, poorly set expectations result in a lack of focus and direction. When priorities are unclear, it becomes challenging to allocate time and energy effectively, leading to diminished productivity and wasted potential. Have you ever been here when you feel like everyone is spinning their wheels and getting nowhere fast? This is what happens often, not just at work but at home too.

So instead of waiting for someone else to place expectations on you, why not set expectations for yourself?

Instead of waiting for someone else to place expectations on you, why not set expectations for yourself?

Setting Expectations for Yourself

As I mentioned early on in this book, many of us spend way too much time waiting for permission to move, shift, change, or even make a decision. Then our experience is formed by others' experience of us and what they expect from us. That is a deflating way to go about life. Alternatively, imagine a world where you choose to set expectations for yourself. Let me repeat that: you imagine a world where you *choose* to set expectations for yourself.

Understanding your job role and responsibilities is crucial for effective self-leadership and career growth. Here are a few techniques to help you identify and clarify your job role.

Job Analysis

Job analysis involves a study of your job to identify its essential duties, responsibilities, and the skills required. This technique helps you gain a clear understanding of your role and how it fits within the organization (Danao 2024). In the context of work, you can't set clear expectations for yourself if you don't know what you are performing against.

Here's a step-by-step breakdown of how to perform a job analysis.

- The first step is to review the roles and responsibilities for your specific position. Interview employees, supervisors, HR personnel, and coworkers to get an idea of your roles, tasks, and responsibilities. Once you come up with a viable list, consider the level of difficulty required for each task or skill set. Rank and organize the specific tasks based on the amount of skill level and experience involved (Danao 2024).

- Check out similar positions to evaluate whether the scope of the job is aligned with industry standards. A good tip is to browse job descriptions for similar positions on LinkedIn or Indeed. You can even check out job descriptions and compensation on Payscale and http://Salary.com (Danao 2024).

- Not every position has the same essential skills, training, and experience. Management could even opt to assign or unassign responsibilities based on their level of importance to the team. As a result, it's important to define the specific skills, training, and education required for each candidate. The more specific you are, the better your job analysis will be (Danao 2024).

- One of the most crucial aspects of a job analysis is looking at compensation and other benefits. What is the salary range for the role? How much are your competitors offering for the same role? What are the skills necessary to move up the salary range (Danao 2024)?

I know this will take a lot of effort on your part, but this is an effort to take back your power. Another way to assess the right job fit that aligns with your values and organizational goals is to seek performance feedback.

Performance Feedback

Seeking regular performance feedback from supervisors, peers, and subordinates provides valuable insights into your job role and responsibilities. This feedback helps you understand how others perceive your performance and identify areas for improvement. I will go into giving and receiving feedback in the next chapter in more depth, but for purposes of clarity in the expectations you have for yourself, it's important to seek regular feedback from your supervisor, team members, and other people at home and work. Be very specific about the aspects of your role you want feedback on. After you receive their feedback, conduct your own self-assessment to identify any discrepancies and areas you need to work on.

By utilizing job analysis and gathering performance feedback, you can gain a clearer understanding of your job role and responsibilities. This clarity is essential for effective self-leadership and career development. It's also going to be critical to having others accept the expectations you set for yourself and not the other way around.

Communicating Your Expectations to Others

Years ago, I remember reading Reid Hoffman's book *The Alliance*, wherein he posited that the traditional employer-employee relationship of long-term loyalty on either side was a thing of the past (Hoffman et al. 2014). Instead, he and his co-authors talked about this idea of an alliance that is formed between employer and employee when, at time of hire and frequently throughout the year, both recalibrate the value and expectations the one has to the other (Hoffman et al. 2014). This might look like the employer telling the employee the specific goals they believe the employee can help them with and the employee telling the employer their length of stay and their goals. If there is alignment on both sides, then an alliance is formed where they meet each other's needs. Then they check in a few times a year to see if the plan still works, and if timelines need to be adjusted (Hoffman et al. 2014).

This concept really stuck with me as I rarely recall this much about a book, having read it as much as 10 years ago. It's because there is a sense of freedom, ownership, and empowerment embedded in the idea. Once you come up with your own expectations for yourself, it's time to communicate your own expectations to those at work and at home. Otherwise, how can you expect them to read your mind and meet something they aren't clear about?

Here are some skills you can focus on to improve your ability to communicate your expectations of yourself effectively: First, you'll want to focus on your ability to articulate to others as clearly as possible what you expect from yourself. This would include things like structure, conciseness, tone, modulation, active listening, and adaptable communication. So if you get tongue-twisted when you go to speak to your manager and are unable to state your position, you will lose their attention. That's why it's worth it to invest in these skills. Second, it is no surprise that you need to do what I described in *The Alliance* – you want to establish regular feedback channels to be sure everyone understands and agrees on the expectations. Finally, you can have expectations all day, but you also need to be sure that the expectations you have for yourself closely align with organizational objectives in the context of work. If not, people may hear you, but won't agree with or support your focus.

Expecting Clear Expectations from Others

Understanding what is expected of you can significantly enhance your performance and satisfaction in your role. When expectations are not clear, it's crucial to proactively seek clarification. You should expect clear expectations and, in a respectful way, hold people accountable for that clarity. In my real-life example at the beginning of this chapter, Joe was waiting for his boss to schedule time to calibrate expectations. Joe could, instead, reach out to his boss and ask

Understanding what is expected of you can significantly enhance your performance and satisfaction in your role.

to schedule 15 minutes to go over priorities and ask the important questions he needs to ask to move forward on projects and begin to feel successful in his role. This would move Joe from frustrated and confused to empowered and purpose-filled.

As you learn to lead yourself from a place of strength and purpose, here are some steps for you to take to seek clarity from those around you:

1. Prepare your questions: Before approaching your manager or peer, prepare specific questions that will help you understand their expectations. Preparation is key to reducing your nerves. Consider asking about deadlines, priorities, and desired outcomes. Maybe even ask them whether they have ever seen what you are about to do NOT go as planned and ask them to describe what happened.

2. Schedule a meeting: Arrange a dedicated time to discuss your questions. This shows that you value their input and are committed to understanding your role. A special tip here is to offer a few times that you already know show open on their calendar to reduce the back-and-forth. Alternatively, if they have an assistant, just go directly to them to schedule.

3. Ask open-ended questions: Use open-ended questions to encourage detailed responses – for example, "Can you elaborate on the key deliverables for this project?" or "What are the top priorities for this task?" This kind of question gets them talking, and that gets you more information and also reveals blind spots and opportunities to shine!

4. Summarize and confirm: After the discussion, summarize what you've understood and confirm it with the person. This ensures that you are both on the same page. To be extra clear, send an email just reiterating the discussion and any due dates for deliverables too. Doing this shows your focus and professionalism. Remember: inward shine, outward brilliance.

Now that you know the steps to gain clarity, let's look at dealing with ambiguity when someone you seek clarity from is either not open or too busy to shed light on timelines or expectations for you.

Dealing with Ambiguity

There is nothing more frustrating than when we are primed and ready to move forward on a project or goal, and those who need to provide direction are unwilling or unavailable to provide us clarity to ensure success. Worse yet, it's also deflating to feel like you can't even get started, because of rapidly shifting priorities, some known and some unknown.

> *It is frustrating when we are primed and ready to move forward but those who need to provide direction are unwilling or unavailable to provide us clarity to ensure success.*

Just before I decided to quit my job and start my own business, I was working in an organization where I was leading customer experience. It was like no position I have ever held in that it would be much harder to improve the customer's experience since the "customers" were residents of a 500,000-person-county. Some of my challenges were that there were many different stakeholders and there was a political undercurrent at play, and it wasn't like I could gather them all together at once to ask their opinion on our service delivery. I was hired to use my creativity to make positive change happen, but other factors out of my control made it hard for me to act upon objectives. One point of confusion was that I felt like I was waiting for the leadership team to give me the green light on many substantial projects, and I often felt like I was in a holding pattern. For someone like me who has an entrepreneurial spirit, it can be hard to slow me down once I get moving forward on achieving goals.

Honestly, it felt stifling. While I did go to my manager with my concerns, it seemed like forever before I obtained clarity, and then I found myself smack in the middle of two reorganizations, which presented a whole different level of ambiguity.

Since that frustrating situation, I learned some strategies that worked to gain more clarity and minimize my frustrations around ambiguous objectives:

- Take initiative: When expectations are not clear, take the initiative to define your own goals and share them with your manager or peers for feedback. This works at home too when conflict can be just as rampant if things aren't clear. Although I know that this can be easier said than done, it takes courage and foresight to seek clarity when we need it.

- Set interim goals: Break down tasks into smaller, more manageable steps with your own deadlines. This approach helps you make progress even in the absence of clear guidance. I learned to do this to begin to feel successful again in my example above, because the big steps I wanted to take were not possible given the organizational changes that were all around.

- Stay flexible: In the previous chapter, you learned a lot about the flexibility required to be successful in our relationships at work and at home. Be prepared to adjust your plans as more information becomes available. Flexibility allows you to adapt to changing expectations and requirements. The senior leaders in your organization will take notice of your willingness to bend.

- Document everything: Keep a record of your tasks, decisions, and any communications regarding expectations. This documentation can help clarify misunderstandings and provide a reference point if needed. If you're assigned a project with vague instructions, outline your understanding of the project and proposed steps, then seek confirmation or adjustments from your supervisor. Be careful not to use this as a weapon to prove you are right in any given situation, but instead let them know that you are serious about getting the details right and moving forward according to agreement.

Something that I learned as a little girl when I felt like I wasn't always clear on my role in my larger family is that I needed to advocate for myself, because no one else could fight for me like I could fight for me. While it is important for me to address this in this chapter, you will see much more of this in the final chapter.

Self-Advocacy

Advocating for yourself is a critical aspect of self-leadership, particularly when faced with ambiguous expectations. It involves asserting your needs and seeking the information necessary to perform your role effectively. If you are staying present for this journey we are on together, you will see that the work that you did in Parts I and II of this book prepared you to advocate for yourself in this way. If you don't understand who you are – your strengths and limitations – it will be hard for you to discover the power you have to show up in these moments that require advocacy.

If you don't understand your strengths and limitations, it will be hard to discover your power to show up in moments that require advocacy.

Let's dive into some ideas to help you move from a potentially passive participant in your own journey to an active one who can advocate for clarity when you need it:

- Be assertive, not aggressive: Communicate your need for clarity in a respectful and assertive manner. Use "I" statements to express how ambiguity affects your work and what you need to move forward. When you do this, you will impress upon those from whom you seek clarity that you take your priorities seriously and want to be sure you get things just right.

- Request regular check-ins: Propose regular check-ins with your manager to discuss progress and any evolving expectations. This proactive approach demonstrates your commitment to meeting their expectations. By the way, regular check-ins work with anyone you are approaching for clarity.

- Use constructive language: Frame your requests in a positive light. Instead of saying, "I don't understand what you want," try "I want to ensure I meet your expectations. Could you please provide more details on . . .?" How we say things is sometimes more important than what we say. You don't want to be perceived as too aggressive or pushy, but professionally persistent when seeking answers to help you move forward on projects.

- Seek resources and support: If direct clarification is not possible, look for other resources or colleagues who can provide insights. Leverage available tools, such as project management software, to organize and track your work. Be careful here that you do not step on the toes of your manager. You might be able to access ideas or help via human resources.

In the journey of self-leadership, expecting clear expectations from others, managing ambiguity, and advocating for yourself are vital skills. By seeking clarity proactively, adopting strategies to handle uncertainty, and confidently advocating for your needs, you can navigate your professional environment more effectively and achieve your goals with greater precision and confidence.

Once you have moved out of the ambiguity zone, you still need to learn how to stay there and even adjust expectations when things change. Let's look at that next.

Maintaining and Adjusting Expectations

I want to remind you of the idea that work and what we do there is not static; it's ever-changing. So we need to be maintaining expectations, and be open to adjusting them for ourselves and others. This means we need to keep a finger on the pulse of our progress both personally and professionally, and decide whether we need to change when circumstances change.

In Chapter 9, I introduced Jennifer Curtain and her openness to changing jobs, even if it meant moving to other cities to do it. In my conversation with her on my podcast, we spoke about an epiphany she had in a previous role when she realized that the leadership team had a "keep-the-status-quo" mindset that did not mesh with hers. Additionally, they were not as focused on creating an inclusive and uplifting culture as she had hoped. So she made the decision to go to another company in a different, more challenging role that allowed her the autonomy to lead in the way that aligned with the expectations that she had for herself as a leader. The role she was in no longer served her. As a result, she chose to lead herself first.

Regularly reviewing ours and others' expectations just means that we stay in sync and can minimize confusion and conflict. The parties involved won't hold grudges or feel taken for granted, because you

> *Regularly reviewing expectations means we stay in sync and can minimize confusion and conflict.*

created a culture that always offered clarity in the midst of chaos. This review will also require that you exercise a bit of self-compassion and forgive yourself for mistakes or oversights on your journey. This consistent review will be a gift for yourself.

As you're reading this, you might be thinking, "Heather, sure I can make adjustments, but how the heck do I manage up or manage the expectations of my boss or my boss's boss when adjustments need to be made?" This can be an intimidating thing to do, so following are a few things I want you to keep in mind.

Managing up involves effectively communicating and working with your direct manager to achieve mutual goals and create a productive working relationship. Here are some tips to help you manage up successfully and make adjustments when necessary:

- Understand their goals and priorities. Knowing what your manager values and prioritizes helps you align your efforts with their expectations and the organization's objectives. If your manager is focused on increasing customer satisfaction, prioritize tasks that directly contribute to improving customer service. If you can find out their communication style – what makes them feel heard and valued – you can make sure that you communicate your new expectations to them in a way that makes them feel good about the direction. Also, engage in conversations to better understand their short-term and long-term goals.

- Be proactive and solutions-oriented. Taking initiative and presenting solutions rather than just problems demonstrates your leadership and problem-solving skills. Think ahead and anticipate what your manager might need or what challenges might arise. Also, when discussing issues, come prepared with potential solutions and recommendations.

For example, if you foresee a potential delay in a project, inform your manager early and suggest alternative plans to keep the project on track.

- Build a trust-centered relationship. I already wrote a lot about trust in Chapter 8, but I want to reiterate that if you want to be successful in your relationship with those higher up in your organization, you need to build trust by always delivering on your commitments, being honest about your capabilities, and remaining ethical and transparent in everything you do. Do not cover up mistakes or challenges, but let others see more of you.

- Adapt to their preferences. I am hesitant to write this because I don't want you to think that you need to adapt so much that you lose a part of yourself. Remember what I said about cognitive flexibility? I just mean that you have to be open to shifting how you operate for how they operate, even just a little, to be sure your relationship grows and stays strong. For example, if your manager prefers quick email updates and not lengthy meetings, then go with the flow. If they preferred detailed reports instead of ones that gloss over facts, adjust that to some degree. Find a middle point whenever possible.

To ensure that you are setting, maintaining, and adjusting expectations you have for yourself or that others have of you, you must lean into the assertiveness, professionalism, and focus that are required to get everyone on the same page. Focus on being trustworthy, adaptable, and comprehensible so that your message is understood from the beginning and you get the alignment you're seeking. In the next chapter, we'll explore some tools to give and receive feedback so that those who need to learn from it will do so.

Bright Ideas for Self-Leadership

Clarity Conversations

Practice seeking clear expectations through structured conversations.

1. **Identify a task:** Choose a task or project where you feel the expectations are unclear.

2. **Prepare questions:** Write down specific questions to ask your manager or peer to gain clarity. For example:
   - What are the key deliverables for this task?
   - What are the priorities and deadlines?
   - How will success be measured?

3. **Schedule a meeting:** Arrange a time to discuss these questions with the relevant person.

4. **Conduct the conversation:** Use active listening and take notes during the discussion.

5. **Summarize and confirm:** After the conversation, summarize your understanding and confirm it with the person.

Role Reversal Exercise

Follow these steps to understand the importance of clear expectations by experiencing the role of a manager or peer.

1. **Partner up:** Pair up with a colleague or friend.

2. **Assign roles:** One person plays the role of a manager, and the other is the employee.

3. **Scenario creation:** The "manager" assigns a task with intentionally vague instructions.

4. **Seek clarity:** The "employee" asks questions to clarify the expectations.

5. **Switch roles:** Repeat the exercise with the role reversed.

Feedback Is a Gift

Have you ever heard that feedback is a gift? While I believe that now, I also know how hard it can be to receive it, especially when it's not all butterflies and rainbows. In Chapter 7, I briefly shared with you about my first 360-degree feedback from many people at work. What I didn't go into detail about was the fact that my manager gave all his direct reports very low scores. While he tried to reassure me that I was the best, I couldn't get past the fact that I was the best of the worst. On my feedback report, I could see that my direct reports seemed to give me glowing scores and remarks, but my colleagues were confused about where I spent my time. It all left me feeling a little battered. Over a period of three months, I processed that report and looked at it often and then decided what I would do to fix what I could. The feedback hurt – a lot – but then it was time to act!

Feedback is the cornerstone of personal growth and workplace empowerment.

Feedback really is the cornerstone of personal growth and workplace empowerment. As someone who is seeking to grow in self-leadership, there is no better way to discover what is inside of you and learn to lead yourself much better than you thought possible. While it can be time-consuming and sometimes painful to receive, if acted upon properly you will grow and stretch to reveal beneath the clay a beautiful golden core.

Self-leadership involves the adeptness at both giving and receiving feedback, which is essential for personal and professional growth. Effective self-leaders understand that constructive feedback helps identify strengths and areas for improvement, fostering continuous development.

Effective self-leaders understand that constructive feedback fosters continuous development.

They are skilled at providing clear, specific, and actionable feedback to others, facilitating mutual growth and better performance within teams. Additionally, they are open to receiving feedback, viewing it as a valuable tool for self-reflection and enhancement. This dual capability enhances communication, builds trust, and creates a culture of continuous improvement and adaptability in any setting.

Why do some people steer clear of giving and receiving feedback, and how does feedback impact our perceptions of our worth that we dug into in Chapter 1? Let's look more at the psychology of feedback.

The Psychology of Feedback

Feedback is a crucial component of self-leadership, yet it often encounters resistance. Understanding the psychological reasons behind this resistance can help in effectively navigating and leveraging feedback for growth. Resistance to feedback can stem from various psychological factors, including fear of criticism, threat to self-esteem, and cognitive dissonance. Individuals may perceive feedback as a personal attack rather than a constructive tool for improvement, leading to defensiveness. Additionally, feedback can evoke feelings of inadequacy and vulnerability, making it difficult for individuals to accept and act on it. Recognizing these underlying reasons can help in creating a more supportive environment where feedback is seen as an opportunity rather than a threat.

Coming Back to Growth Mindset

As I addressed in Chapter 9, "Leaning into Flexible Thinking," the concept of a growth mindset, introduced by Carol Dweck, is closely linked to the ability to accept feedback and pursue continuous improvement. A growth mindset is the belief that abilities and intelligence can be developed through dedication and hard work. Individuals with a growth mindset view feedback as a valuable resource for learning and development. They are more likely to embrace challenges, persist in the face of setbacks, and see effort as a path to mastery. By cultivating a growth mindset, individuals can transform feedback into actionable insights that drive personal and professional growth (Dweck 2006). This happened to me after receiving that dramatic feedback from the 360-degree feedback I mentioned earlier. I was in a fixed mindset state for a little while after receiving that feedback. I felt like I had been given a one-two punch to the stomach, but then I reframed the feedback and transitioned into the growth mindset. I knew that I could learn from it and grow as a result.

I'll share some strategies a little later in this chapter regarding how to bounce back more quickly from constructive or even negative feedback. Next, let's look at how feedback you receive might impact your perception of yourself and, most likely, your sense of self-worth.

Feedback and Self-Perception

Feedback plays a significant role in shaping and refining self-perception and self-awareness. It serves as a mirror, reflecting how others perceive our actions, behaviors, and performance. While feedback can sometimes challenge your self-perception by highlighting areas that need improvement, it also provides an opportunity to gain a more accurate and holistic understanding of yourself, which connects us back to our work in Part I of this book on self-understanding. This process of receiving and integrating feedback can enhance your self-awareness, enabling you to recognize blind spots and align your self-perception with reality. In turn, this refined self-awareness can lead to more effective self-leadership, as you become better equipped to leverage your strengths and address your weaknesses.

Receiving and integrating feedback can enhance self-awareness, enabling you to align your self-perception with reality.

By understanding the psychological reasons behind resistance to feedback, linking it to a growth mindset, and recognizing its impact on self-perception, you can enhance your self-leadership capabilities. Embracing feedback as a tool for growth fosters a culture of continuous improvement and personal development. Now I'd like to look more closely at the art of giving feedback.

The Art of Giving Feedback

I do believe that giving feedback is an art, but with a little science too. While I am going to give you some ideas on how to provide others with feedback, I am going to dispel some myths about what is required to do it well and leave people with dignity in the process.

Principles of Effective Feedback

Effective feedback has specific characteristics that make it useful and actionable. By adhering to these principles, you can ensure that your feedback contributes positively to the recipient's growth. Keep in mind that these principles and any of the strategies I share apply to positive, constructive, and even negative feedback:

- Must be specific: Feedback should be clear and specific, addressing the person's particular behaviors or actions rather than giving them vague generalizations. This helps the recipient understand exactly what needs improvement and what they did well. Instead of saying, "You need to improve your presentations," say, "In your last presentation, the slides were well organized, but the key points could be more clearly highlighted to keep your audience engaged." If you are not specific, the person on the other end flails a bit until they can uncover exactly what to do next.

- Must be actionable: Feedback should provide concrete suggestions for improvement or reinforcement. This makes it easier for the recipient to take practical steps based on the feedback. Provide clear next steps: "To improve your presentations, try using bullet points to highlight key points and practicing in front of a colleague to refine your delivery." Can you see how this specificity can help those on the other end of your feedback receive it and act upon it?

- Must be timely: Giving feedback promptly ensures that the context and details are fresh in both the giver's and the receiver's minds. This increases the relevance and impact of the feedback. Offer feedback soon after the observed behavior: "I'd like to discuss your presentation skills now while the details are still fresh."

I stated this in Chapter 8, but it's worth highlighting that not all feedback is negative. In fact, I think we need to create cultures where all feedback is promoted, nurtured, and celebrated. If we could look forward to positive accolades as much as we do constructive feedback, we would all learn to grow faster in self-leadership. Lean into giving people positive feedback often, which makes them more receptive to constructive feedback. I have

Lean into giving people positive feedback often, which makes them more receptive to constructive feedback.

been a leader of people (in addition to myself and my own children) for over two decades. I have been very liberal in spotting and then recognizing people on my team, because I know it makes them feel valued and I am proud of their efforts and results. Since I always focus so much time on this type of recognition, when I do need to sit down with them to help them see a better way with constructive dialogue, they accept that feedback. They know I am in it with them to win at life and at work, so they don't hesitate to listen and act accordingly.

Now that you know the nuts and bolts of what is required at the foundation of feedback, let's look at delivering feedback that not only informs, but leaves the recipient of your feedback in a much better position to learn and grow. Although many of my examples are work-related and delivered to someone who might report to a manager, in many ways the approaches I share here can be adapted to discussions at home with your spouse, children, and others.

Techniques for Delivery

Delivering feedback effectively requires a thoughtful approach that encourages engagement and minimizes defensiveness. I want to have you think differently and less robotically about the feedback delivery process. I know that we have been taught the *sandwich method*, wherein you are supposed to start with a positive comment, then give your negative or constructive comment, and then end on a positive note. I don't agree with this rigid approach. In fact, the one thing I know to be true is that it signals to the person receiving feedback that, right after that positive comment, they are about to hear something potentially painful, stopping them from truly hearing the feedback.

I understand that the world wants a formula for everything, and while I am a big believer in making things easier, I also think that we need to understand that feedback is a gift that shows that we care about the person or people on the other end. If we do it in the right way our brilliance shines through *and* we help the other remove the clay of being so-so. As such, let's move away from a robotic, check-the-box way of giving feedback to one that leans into the heart and gift we are, in fact, giving them.

Here are some techniques to help you deliver feedback constructively and from a place of care and concern:

- Use "I" statements: I mentioned this technique in the previous chapter, because it works. Using "I" statements focuses on your observations and feelings rather than making the feedback sound accusatory. Instead of saying, "You never listen in meetings," say, "I feel that during meetings, some key points might be getting missed because there are frequent interruptions." Then I would go further to say, "How can we work together to ensure interruptions are minimized so we can all get on the same page?" This last step feels like a partnership instead of something the recipient has to think about and do all alone.

- Focus on behavior, not the person: Address specific behaviors rather than making it about the person's character. This reduces defensiveness and keeps the feedback constructive. Instead of saying, "You're disorganized," say, "I've noticed that the last few reports have been submitted late. Let's discuss how we can improve the process."

- Understand their perspective: Before giving feedback, try to understand the recipient's viewpoint and any potential challenges they might be facing. Ask questions to gather context: "I noticed the reports were delayed. Is there something that's been making it difficult to meet the deadlines?" This sort of question gets them to talk to you. There might be more you can do to show them you care about them. This shows them that you are empathetic.

- Show genuine concern: Self-leadership is one element of Caring Leadership, which I write and speak about often. I define Caring Leadership as showing concern and kindness toward those who look to you for guidance in some way. Whether it's your manager, your team member, your coworker, your child or family members, when you express your feedback with a genuine interest in the recipient's development and well-being, you show that you care. Frame your feedback within the context of their growth: "I'm sharing this feedback because I believe it will help you progress in your role and achieve your goals."

- Be supportive: Offer your support and help them find solutions to the issues discussed. Suggest ways you can assist: "How can I support you in organizing your workload better?" Some years ago, one of my team members was a team lead whom I witnessed act beneath her natural leadership style in an email exchange with another coworker. Shortly after, I asked to speak with her to inquire about why her email exchange was so abrupt with that coworker. It was very uncharacteristic of how she showed up and I told her so. She explained how she was feeling about the other team member and other exchanges that took place outside of this email to provide context. While I worked to understand her perspective, I also coached her on what she could do to mend the fence with her coworker. She appreciated that I challenged her to be her best self and supported her in the process.

While this isn't a check-the-box approach to delivering feedback, if you take these strategies to heart and use them in a genuine way, the person on the other end will know it's coming from a place of you wanting to help them continue to remove their own clay and reveal their greatness. That's when the relationship between you and them grows to a new level!

Now that you know the best way to deliver the feedback, let's focus on how to apply what you know in a methodical way.

Practical Application

To integrate these principles, techniques, and the empathetic approach into your feedback practice, consider these three things: prepare beforehand, continue to practice active listening, and follow up after the feedback.

Giving feedback, especially if it's constructive in nature, can make us nervous. I know I experience nervousness beforehand, mostly because I really want the recipient to know, first and foremost, that I care. That is why preparing to give feedback is so important. Take time to gather your thoughts, focus on specific behaviors, and plan your approach to ensure the feedback is clear and constructive with a touch of heart.

As I am sure you already gathered, I believe that practicing active listening is one of the most important things we can do to sustain long-term relationships. Shoot, I wrote a whole book on it! As you are working to comprehend what might be happening to someone, really seek to understand the other person's responses and show empathy toward their perspective. This

Seek to understand the other person's responses and show empathy toward their perspective.

means that you have to go into your interactions or feedback sessions with a service mindset. Are you there to serve them with the feedback, or is it somehow self-serving? When they know that it is the former that motivates you, you build trust with them.

Once you have delivered the feedback, schedule follow-up meetings to review progress and provide ongoing support. This shows your commitment to their development and reinforces the feedback. Going back to my example with my team member and her coworker, I followed up with her after she decided to take that team member to lunch to find common ground. I wanted to see how it went and what I could do to help that relationship continue to improve. She disclosed that it was getting better, and that their relationship is still a work in progress.

By adhering to these principles, employing effective delivery techniques, and maintaining an empathetic approach, you can turn feedback into a powerful gift that fosters growth, enhances performance, and strengthens your relationships.

Let's look deeper at the skill of being on the receiving end of the feedback. Remember, all feedback is a gift. Not every piece of feedback requires action, but it does require our consideration, or what I call decoding.

The Skill of Receiving Feedback

In Chapter 8, I touched on active listening and my five-step proprietary approach, called the *Cycle of Active Listening* (Figure 11.1). In the context of receiving feedback, this type of listening is the only way to really hear what the other person wants you to know

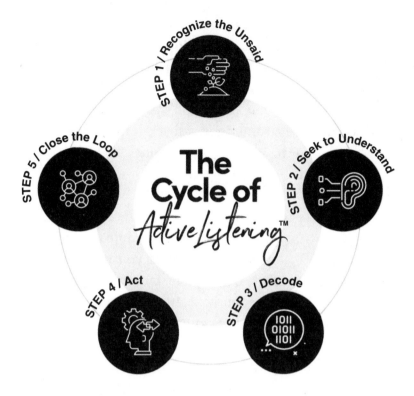

FIGURE 11.1 The Cycle of Active Listening.

Source: Copyright Employee Fanatix and Heather Younger.

and potentially do about what they are telling you. If you start off taking part in any feedback session with the mindset "This is a gift," you are already in the right mindset to listen well.

Without reiterating all the steps to active listening, I want to focus on the steps **decode**, **act**, and **close the loop**, because they work closely together.

Let's assume you have just received feedback from someone and now you want to take time to

> *If you start off a feedback session with the mindset "This is a gift," you are already in the right mindset to listen well.*

think it through. Let's also assume that the person will allow you the time to reflect before fully responding. When we decode feedback, we break down what was said and process what it means. If we are diligent, we might look at our past performance or talk with others who know us, not in a gossipy way, but to validate or give texture to the feedback. To this point, make sure to talk to people who you know won't pander to your need not to feel discomfort regarding the feedback. They will be kind and will also guide you to see how the original feedback may have been accurate and show you the nuances of where the feedback might not be on point.

Once you have taken a reasonable amount of time to **decode** what you heard from the other person, schedule time to sit down with them again to let them know what you think about their feedback, what you plan to **do** about it, if anything, and then **close the loop** with them on your efforts to address their concerns or suggestions. Now they know that you have heard them and take their feedback seriously. You can take it one step further and **close the loop** again a few months later to see if your performance or behaviors have changed in their opinion and seek even more feedback. Can you see how this simple process works to get you the most out of the feedback while also leaving the person providing you the feedback feeling heard?

Let's assume you are in a meeting where you don't have much time to decode outside of the meeting. For example, what if you are being reprimanded by someone, and you need to respond on the spot? I would still use these words to defer an in-depth response after you have had time to process it all. "Thank you so much for this feedback. I can see how critical this issue is and even the impact I have had on xyz, which I take very seriously. Because this is so important, do you mind if I process this and come back to you by the end of the day with what I plan to do about it?" Remember, you want to land on the right result and keep your relationship intact, so you wouldn't want to rush your response if you can at all help it.

One important note when it comes to receiving feedback is to separate the critique of your actions or results you receive from who you are and your self-worth. Again, I know that this is easier said than done. You have learned a lot about me in this book and you know that is an area of constant struggle for me. Here are a few tips I use that can also help you protect yourself from the feedback you receive:

- Focus on specific behaviors, not personal identity. When receiving feedback, concentrate on the specific actions or behaviors being discussed rather than viewing it as a judgment of your character. Understand that feedback is aimed at improving your performance, not defining who you are as a person. Instead of thinking, "I'm not good at my job," reframe it as "I need to improve my presentation skills, and that is something I can control."

  Understand that feedback is aimed at improving your performance, not defining who you are as a person.

- Practice self-compassion. Just as I mentioned earlier about showing concern and kindness to others when you are giving them feedback, treat yourself with that same kindness and understanding when receiving feedback. Acknowledge that making mistakes and needing improvement is part of being human. Remind yourself that your worth is not determined by a single performance or critique. Instead of harshly criticizing yourself, say, "It's okay to make mistakes. I am learning and improving every day."

These tips can help you maintain a healthy perspective on feedback, ensuring it serves as a constructive tool for growing in self-leadership rather than a blow to your self-worth.

You will encounter instances where the feedback you receive is very challenging either in how it's delivered or the topic they are addressing. I will focus on that next.

Overcoming Challenges in Feedback

Negative feedback can be challenging, especially when it is harsh, unconstructive, or inaccurate. However, learning to handle such feedback effectively is a crucial aspect of self-leadership. While much of what I shared in the previous section still applies here, and I will note that, there are nuances to address when things get heated.

First, stay calm and composed. When you receive negative feedback, your initial reaction might be defensive or emotional. Take a deep breath and try to stay calm. Responding with composure allows you to process the feedback rationally.

Here are some specific steps you can take in this situation:

- Pause before responding: Take a moment to collect your thoughts before reacting. This helps prevent impulsive or emotional responses.

- Ask clarifying questions: If the feedback is vague or seems unconstructive, ask for specific examples to understand the issues better.

- Seek to understand: Try to understand the perspective of the person giving the feedback, even if you disagree with it. This can provide valuable insights into how others perceive your actions. For example, if a colleague says, "Your reports are always incomplete," ask, "Can you provide specific instances where the reports were incomplete and what information was missing?"

Remember, you need to seek to serve the other by your presence even when it is painful. You will get more out of the interaction when you have the service mindset anyway. If you go in the interaction to be "right," you will just anger the other person. It will also be hard for you to receive any value in the feedback, and there is always value to be found in feedback.

Second, evaluate the feedback objectively, which just means to decode what you heard. Not all feedback is accurate or fair. Try to assess the feedback objectively to determine its validity by doing the following. First, consider whether there is any truth to the feedback, even if it was delivered harshly. Look for any constructive elements that you can use to improve. Next, if you're unsure about the accuracy of the feedback, seek input from other trusted colleagues or mentors. This is still a part of the decoding phase, because decoding can be done alone or with others. Finally, determine what actions, if any, you will take based on the feedback. If the feedback is inaccurate, you may choose to disregard it, but still look for any underlying issues that might be addressed. This is a critical point to make, because I have found that there will always be at least a small grain of truth in even the most hurtful feedback. When you return to the person who provided the feedback with a semblance of compromise or an openness to change just a little, you leave them feeling heard. You might also be able to save the relationship in the process.

I have found that there will always be at least a small grain of truth in even the most hurtful feedback.

Let me share a personal example with you. About two decades ago, I received some harsh feedback in a letter a friend wrote to me about how she perceived me. The letter was very hurtful and went into detail about relationships with some of our other friends and my journey since we were in school together. Much like that awful 360-degree feedback survey I received from my boss in the story I told earlier, I held on to the letter for a long while before I could move past it. Shortly after I read that letter,

I reached out to her to let her know I received it and how hurtful it was. That conversation didn't go well, and we didn't speak for some time. Honestly, I wasn't ready to own any of what she stated in the letter. However, once months went by, I decided that I needed to decide what to keep and what to throw away regarding her feedback. As I took some time with it, I realized there were some grains of truth that I needed to work on and acknowledge. A long while later, she and I mended our relationship and talked about this information. I never forgot about the sting of the letter, but I do think I have adjusted how I show up as a result.

Third, if feedback is particularly harsh or unconstructive, it's important to address it professionally by, first, discussing it constructively. If the feedback is not helpful, discuss it with the giver and express your need for constructive criticism. Frame it positively by stating your desire to improve and asking for specific suggestions. For example, "I appreciate your feedback and want to improve. Could you provide specific examples and suggestions for how I can do better?" Consider documenting the interaction, especially if it is a workplace issue, because you don't want this to be a recurring concern. This will also help you be able to address it with HR later, if needed.

When navigating sensitive situations and feedback, there are a few things to keep in mind to ensure the best outcome:

- If we want to do anything well, we must first prepare. In this case, prepare yourself mentally and emotionally for a sensitive conversation. This means you should be clear about the purpose of the feedback and what you hope to achieve, and at the same time put yourself in the other person's shoes to understand their perspective and potential reactions. For example, if you need to give critical feedback to a team member or coworker about their performance, consider how they might feel and plan your approach accordingly.

- If you want the person to whom you are providing feedback to be able to leave the interaction with their dignity in hand and with the relationship intact, ensure that the feedback session is conducted in a safe and private environment. This means that you should select a private and comfortable setting for the discussion, and keep the feedback session confidential.

As discussed above, closing the loop on feedback and setting up regular feedback opportunities is essential for ongoing development and improvement. It helps in maintaining open lines of communication and fosters a culture of continuous learning. Handling negative feedback, navigating sensitive situations, and creating a continuous feedback loop are crucial components of self-leadership.

Bright Ideas for Self-Leadership

Go to http://Caringleadershiplearning.com/feedback-assessment to take an assessment on your feedback style and get some development tips on how to improve.

- **Feedback Journal:** Use this to track and reflect on feedback received and given, fostering continuous improvement.
  - Set up a journal: Create a dedicated feedback journal, either digitally or in a notebook.
  - Document feedback: Each time you receive feedback, note the date, source, and content of the feedback. Reflect on how you felt receiving it and what actions you plan to take.
  - Review regularly: At the end of each week or month, review your entries to identify common themes and areas for growth.
  - Track progress: Note any changes or improvements you've made as a result of the feedback.

- **Feedback Reflection Exercise:** This helps to deepen understanding of personal feedback tendencies and areas for growth.

  - Reflect on past feedback: Think about a recent piece of feedback you received that was difficult to accept. Reflect on why it was challenging and what your initial reaction was.
  - Analyze your response: Consider how you responded to the feedback. Did you react defensively, or did you seek to understand and improve?
  - Plan for improvement: Write down specific steps you can take to handle similar feedback more constructively in the future.
  - Seek additional feedback: Follow up with the person who gave you the original feedback and ask for additional feedback on your progress.

12

Use Your Voice and Be Seen

It's not lost on me that I chose my final chapter to be on using your voice to be seen, given my personal story as a child of not always feeling seen or like my voice didn't matter to some of the adults in my life. The fact is that I have spent the majority of my working life advocating for someone's voice to be heard, whether it's with customers, friends, coworkers, or employees. I wrote an entire book on this topic, and I speak around the world teaching people how to listen well. I have always felt a little like an underdog, and always felt called to fight for those who don't have a voice. Now I am leaning in to tell you to take your voice back. Stand up and be seen for the brilliant person you are. Don't wait for someone else to give you a voice. Also, just as I have spent much of this book showing you how to listen to others, I want you to listen to yourself first.

Whether we are talking about your personal or professional life, your voice is uniquely yours. There is a tremendous power in

When you use your voice, you will experience greater empowerment, engagement, recognition, and overall life satisfaction.

being heard and seen. It is also very liberating to hear your own internal voice. When you use your voice, you will experience greater empowerment, engagement, recognition, and overall life satisfaction. You will no longer hold yourself hostage to others directing your every move, but grow in confidence that you know what your next move should be.

In this chapter I want to help you rediscover your voice and learn to use it to increase your visibility, improve your opportunities, and overcome any barriers along the way. Let's start at the most important part: finding and listening to your own voice.

Finding Your Voice

In the journey of self-leadership, using your voice and being seen are fundamental aspects that empower you to influence others and assert your presence. This section will guide you through the process of self-discovery, overcoming fears, and embracing authenticity to use your voice effectively inside and outside of work.

Before you can effectively use your voice, it's essential to understand what you want your voice to represent. This involves reflecting on your values, expertise, and the impact you wish to have.

Your values are the core principles that guide your decisions and actions. Reflecting on your values helps you determine what is most important to you and what you stand for. Consider doing these two activities to come up with your core values:

1. List your top five values. These could be integrity, compassion, innovation, respect, or any other principles that resonate with you.

2. Consider how your daily actions align with these values. Are there areas where you could better align your behavior with your values?

For example, if integrity is a core value, think about how you can consistently demonstrate honesty in your communications and actions. You will most likely discover some gaps between what you think you value and your actual behaviors. Don't beat yourself up for the gaps, but use the insight as an opportunity to learn and adjust.

In order to use your voice, you need to make sure your voice reflects your expertise. Understanding your areas of expertise allows you to confidently share your knowledge and insights. Here are a few things to consider and evaluate to be able to recognize and leverage your expertise:

1. Write down your top skills and areas of expertise. What do people frequently seek your advice on? You can find some of your skills on LinkedIn if you are active there. People have most likely recognized your top skills there. You could also ask some of your friends and colleagues what they most value about you and that will help you land on your expertise.

2. Identify opportunities to share your expertise, such as writing articles, giving presentations, or mentoring others. For example, if you are skilled in project management, consider offering to lead a workshop or mentor junior colleagues in this area. If people accept your offer, they most likely see you as an expert in that area. That can be a validator for you.

To really leverage your own voice, you need to define the impact you want to have at work and in the broader world. What kind of impact do you want to have? What if you took the time to define what impact you want to have at work, at home, and in your community? It could be things like fostering a positive team culture, driving innovation, or supporting a cause you care about. Once you determine the impact you want to have, *do something* to move yourself closer to those goals.

Let me share a great case study with you that I learned about on my *Leadership With Heart* podcast. This entrepreneur really does illustrate not only the concept of uncovering and using your expertise, but also someone who defined and owned the impact he wanted to have.

Case Study

Antonio McBroom

Antonio McBroom went to college on a scholarship and needed to provide financial support for his aging grandmother, who was still at home. Seeking a job during college orientation, he noticed a "Now hiring" sign at the Ben & Jerry's store and decided to apply, since he already had a love of ice cream. Antonio was hired as a "scooper" and balanced that with his college requirements. Once he got to his sophomore year, he was promoted to shift leader, gaining the responsibility of opening and closing the store. By his junior year, Antonio was the assistant manager, had completed an internship, and was contemplating combining his passion for education and entrepreneurship into his work.

Antonio approached the store owner to inquire about purchasing the store from him before he graduated from college. Despite initial skepticism, they began serious discussions about the requirements for ownership. Then Antonio partnered with a mentor and friend to explore the feasibility of the purchase.

Antonio successfully negotiated the purchase of the Ben & Jerry's store, completing the acquisition two days before college graduation.

Expansion and Challenges: Growing a Multi-Unit Operation

Expansion:

- Antonio expanded from one store to two, then to four, and eventually to seven stores.
- He encountered challenges typical of multi-unit operations, including maintaining consistent standards and managing a larger workforce.

Strategy:

- Antonio studied successful companies like Starbucks for inspiration on maintaining quality and consistency across multiple locations.
- He developed systems and leveraged a team approach to manage the growing number of stores effectively.

Innovation and Community Focus: Partnering with Starbucks

New Opportunity:

- During the pandemic, Antonio observed Starbucks' commitment to supporting Black communities through the creation of community stores featuring Black-inspired art and employing Black contractors.
- He gained recognition for leading a company with majority people of color that delivered exceptional outcomes in the Ben & Jerry's space.

Consulting and Transition:

- Antonio engaged in consulting work with Starbucks, deepening an appreciation for the brand and its values.

- He initiated discussions about becoming a Starbucks operator, leading to a role as a licensed developer for the company.

Key Takeaways:

- Self-discovery and determination: Understanding one's values and goals is crucial in making career decisions that align with personal aspirations and family needs.

- Overcoming challenges: Navigating financial and operational challenges requires strategic thinking, adaptability, and a willingness to ask bold questions.

- Leveraging opportunities: Recognizing and seizing opportunities, such as consulting roles and partnerships, can lead to significant career advancements and business growth.

Antonio's example perfectly illustrates so many elements of self-leadership. Through knowing the impact he wanted, using his voice to pursue his goal, strategic decision-making, seeking mentorship, and embracing opportunities, he navigated challenges and expanded his business, ultimately partnering with a respected global brand to further his entrepreneurial journey. While he had many opportunities to give up, place blame, or wait for others to give him the green light, he fully leveraged his internal shine, tore away his outer clay, and seized the opportunity to get what he wanted and more.

Overcoming Fear

I wrote in Chapter 3 about the role of fear in our lives, and it applies here as well. Fear is a common barrier that prevents many from speaking up and using their voices. Overcoming these fears is crucial for effective self-leadership. The most common fears related to speaking up include fear of judgment, fear of failure, and fear of rejection. I have been there. I remember sitting in many meetings where the fear of judgment and even rejection of my ideas stopped me from piping up. This all points to a lack of psychological safety in the room and in the culture.

Having said that, there are a couple steps we can take to help us bypass that fear and use our voices:

1. Acknowledge your fears: Identify the specific fears that hold you back. Understanding your fears is the first step toward overcoming them. Open up a journal if you need to and take some time to think about where it comes from.

2. Challenge negative thoughts: Replace negative thoughts with positive affirmations. Remind yourself of past successes and your ability to handle challenges. You can revisit Chapter 3 to remind yourself of the steps to reframe a negative into a more positive learning experience.

Earlier this year, I was walking on the track in my gym when a woman stopped me to tell me I was walking the wrong way. I had my airpods in and was focused on listening to an audio book, so her tap on my shoulder startled me. When she spoke again, she said, "We are all walking in this direction. Today is Wednesday." Now, at this point, I am totally lost. Then she said, "There is a sign when you enter the track. Today is Wednesday." I politely shook my head, but I was sort of irritated. First, why do they switch the directions, and why does everyone have to comply? Also, how did I not see any signs since I have walked this track many times before? So I finished my walk and left.

The next day, I walked up the stairs to the track, looking for this sign she spoke of, and there they were, a few tiny 8½-by-11-inch sheets of paper scattered on the rails around a massive track. I had never even noticed them. How could I when they were so small and nondescript? Why wouldn't they put up larger signs that are easier to see? That got me thinking about how many times we fail to directly communicate our needs or opinions to others and they miss it. We put up tiny signs, but don't specifically state our views so others can understand us. We might do this for fear of rejection or judgment, but if we don't speak up, many people will never notice the signs.

For example, if you fear judgment, remind yourself of times when you spoke up and received positive feedback. For the last three years, my team member Ashley would challenge me via Slack, email, and on team meetings. She was never disrespectful, but she was eager to share her insight and intuition. I looked at it as a valuable thing, because it caused me to pause long enough to think through the decision I thought I made. Often I would change my mind, because her reasoning was logical and non-emotional. Interestingly, Ashley is in her 20s and seemed fearless when it came to questioning authority and her right to speak up in the world. Even if she feared speaking up, she had plenty of examples of how, when she did, she learned of the power in her voice.

Ashley is a powerful example of the confidence it takes to know that our voices are worth using. Building confidence can help you overcome fear as well. The two most important things to focus on to build that confidence are to prepare and to take baby steps. On the preparation front, when you think you want to speak up on a topic, prepare your points in advance and then practice delivering the points in a room or to your manager. This is no different than what I need to do before stepping on a stage to speak and inspire hundreds or thousands of leaders: prepare, prepare, prepare. On the "start small" point, when we begin by taking little risks and then gradually increase to speaking up on bigger topics or in a bigger room, we feel more comfortable.

I want to add a special note here for those who manage people. You have not just the authority, but the power to make people feel safe in a room. Think about doing these three things to increase the safety and improve the chances of your team speaking up more often:

- Speak last. When I interviewed communications expert Andy Boian on my podcast, he gave that advice, because that is what he adopted with his team and got really good results. Andy speaks last, because he recognized that his team was hesitant to speak in opposition to something he might say if he spoke first. He realized his power and used it to empower others to speak first.

- Invite people to speak. When you are sitting around a table, pay attention to the unspoken cues that someone wants to share a different view. Then invite them to share, and validate what they say by responding, "Thank you, Joe. That is an interesting way to see the situation." You can either offer to talk it over in private or open it for discussion at the table, which lets Joe know you value his input.

- Confer with them in advance. Sometimes all it takes is for you to discuss in private an idea you know one of your team members has, and then ask them to bring it up in the larger meeting and assure them that you will support the discussion. This increases the feeling of safety and reduces their fear of rejection.

- Recognize their courage. Once someone speaks up in the room, acknowledge the value that they consistently bring to a discussion. For example, after Joe speaks up to share his idea, you could say, "Joe, what a great idea. Although you don't speak up as much, whenever you do, it's brilliant. Share more of your ideas with us, Joe!" He is thrilled and you have also created more safety for others too.

- Foster an alliance. This is a strategy that creates safety and also makes people feel like they are not alone. So Joe speaks up to share his idea in a meeting. You love the idea and recognize it. Then you say, "Evelyn, I know that you and Joe are aligned on this topic. Could you two work together to prepare a brief on this and a budget for this new project?" Now Evelyn and Joe forge a deeper bond of trust.

If you manage even just one person, know that you have more power than you think to make them feel safe and foster an environment where everyone speaks up. Now that we understand what we can do to overcome our own fear of speaking up and help others do the same, let's look at the role of authenticity in helping you use your voice effectively.

Being Your Authentic Self

Authenticity is crucial for using your voice effectively. When you speak authentically, you build trust and connect more deeply with others. The key is to be true to yourself and express your genuine thoughts and feelings. Think about it: when you speak from the heart, even if the viewpoint differs from the majority, you feel in alignment with who you are. This alignment also acts as a persuasive tool to bring people along with you in your thought process. If you try to mimic someone else's style or opinion, people can sense it and you lose trust. Know that your unique perspective is valuable. For example, if you disagree with a proposed strategy, respectfully share your concerns and offer alternative solutions instead of going along with the crowd.

If you try to mimic someone else's style or opinion, people can sense it and you lose trust.

Being authentic also means being willing to show vulnerability. This can strengthen your connections with others and enhance your influence. Don't be afraid to share your failures and what you've learned from them. This shows humility and a willingness to grow. I know that this can be hard, especially given what I wrote about being in unsafe environments, but remember that when you speak up and share, you give others permission to do the same. Who could be more afraid than you in the room and on a given topic? If you are a manager, during a team meeting, share a time when you faced a challenge and how you overcame it. Invite others to share their experiences as well.

Using your voice and being seen are essential components of self-leadership. Through self-discovery, overcoming fears, and embracing authenticity, you can effectively assert your presence and influence others. By reflecting on your values and expertise, addressing common fears, and staying true to yourself, you will enhance your ability to lead and inspire those around you.

One of the main ways of being seen in any environment, but especially at work and in your community, is to increase your visibility.

Increasing Visibility

In the journey of self-leadership, actively participating in your professional environment is crucial. This section will guide you on how to take on visible roles, build a strong professional network, and develop a personal brand that highlights your unique skills and contributions.

Taking on Visible Roles

Active participation in meetings, projects, and public forums is essential for being seen and heard within your organization. It demonstrates your commitment, enhances your visibility, and positions you as a proactive leader. Often, if people don't see or hear you, you are not top of mind. I am speaking from experience here. I am not a very loud person. I am more outgoing than the quiet person, but I don't speak unless I have something additional to add or share. This often makes people wonder if either something is the matter with me, I am angry, or I am just unaware of the conversation that is taking place. I am not advising that you talk for the sake of talking, but I am saying don't assume that your using your voice to echo what is being said in the room has no validity. It has a double benefit: people will keep you top of mind when opportunities arise, and they will respect that you have the courage to speak up at all.

Here are some ways to make sure you are not forgotten at work and are thought of as a key person of influence:

- Volunteer for or take on key projects: Take initiative by volunteering for high-visibility projects. This shows your willingness to contribute and take on responsibilities. I remember when the CEO of my organization asked me to lead a diversity, inclusion, and belonging council at my job. Although I hadn't facilitated this type of group before and I wasn't sure I could do it justice, I still agreed to take on the role. It challenged me to see the different perspectives around the table and make sure to bring them to the surface in our discussions. I'm not sure why the CEO chose me for the role, but no matter; I grew a lot by doing so and proved I would step in when he needed me.

- Prepare to speak up in meetings: I just mentioned that it's a good thing to share your ideas, ask questions, and provide feedback during meetings. This demonstrates your engagement and willingness to contribute, but I want to add that, as I have highlighted often in this book, you should get in the habit of preparing talking points before meetings to ensure you have valuable input ready to share. You will also be less nervous when you do.

- Present your work: Look for opportunities to present your work or findings in team meetings or larger forums. This helps you build confidence and gain recognition for your efforts. When you are intentional in this way, you are more likely to get the results you're seeking versus just winging it when you get in the room.

Consider the story of Jenna. In a mid-sized tech company, Jenna was a talented software developer known for her innovative solutions and meticulous work. However, Jenna was naturally introverted and often reluctant to present her ideas in team meetings or larger forums. She preferred to work quietly and let her results speak for themselves. Despite her valuable contributions, Jenna's reluctance to present her work meant that many of her ideas went unnoticed by senior management.

During a major product development cycle, the company faced a significant challenge: improving the performance and user experience of their flagship software. Various teams were brainstorming solutions, but progress was slow. Jenna had developed a unique approach to optimize the software's performance, but she was hesitant to share it in a high-stakes meeting with senior executives and cross-functional team leaders.

Jenna's immediate supervisor, Mark, recognized the potential impact of her solution. He encouraged her to present her findings at the next all-hands meeting. Jenna was initially reluctant, fearing her idea might not be well received or that she might not effectively communicate its value.

To support her, Mark helped Jenna prepare for the presentation. They worked together to distill the core points of her solution, focusing on its benefits and the specific improvements it would bring. Jenna developed clear and concise slides that illustrated the technical aspects of her proposal, making it easier for nontechnical stakeholders to understand. Mark arranged for several practice sessions where Jenna could rehearse her presentation in front of a small, supportive audience. This helped her build confidence and refine her delivery.

On the day of the all-hands meeting, Jenna felt nervous but prepared. She presented her solution methodically, explaining the technical details and the projected performance improvements. She also included a demo to visually demonstrate the enhancements.

Jenna's presentation was a success. Her solution was not only well received but also sparked a productive discussion among the senior executives and team leaders. They appreciated her thorough analysis and the tangible improvements she demonstrated.

As a result, the company decided to implement Jenna's solution as part of the next software update. Her idea became a cornerstone of the product's performance optimization strategy. Jenna gained significant recognition within the company. Her successful presentation showcased her expertise and potential, leading to increased visibility among senior management. Jenna's willingness to step out of her comfort zone and present her work opened new opportunities for her. She was later promoted to a lead developer role, where she could influence more significant projects and mentor junior colleagues.

What can we learn from Jenna? How can we find more courage to share our unique views and work to improve the places we work and spend our time?

Building a Professional Network

Building a strong professional network is vital for career growth. It opens up opportunities for collaboration, mentorship, and career advancement, both within and outside your organization. It also makes it easier to rebound when you suffer a career setback. Building a professional network can seem daunting, but like anything else worth getting, we need to take small steps to make it happen. Consider taking some of these steps to building your network:

- Attend industry events. Participate in conferences, seminars, and workshops related to your field. These events provide opportunities to meet professionals with similar interests and expand your network. For example, sign up to attend an industry conference and actively engage with speakers and attendees during networking sessions. I would even put out an announcement of your attendance on your social media and see who else is attending this event and then arrange to meet up with them when you're there.

- Join professional organizations. Become a member of professional associations or groups that align with your career interests. This allows you to connect with peers and stay updated on industry trends. For example, you could join a local chapter of a relevant professional association and attend their regular meetings and events. Then be intentional about meeting certain people who are in the room to make sure your time is well spent. Be careful here. This can get expensive. So pay attention throughout the year, because often organizations have member drives when they offer discounts.

- Leverage social media. Use platforms like LinkedIn to connect with colleagues, industry leaders, and potential mentors. Share content, participate in discussions, and showcase your expertise. For example, post insightful articles on LinkedIn and engage with content shared by your network to build your online presence. This might seem overwhelming, but this is how I built my LinkedIn network over time. I have just committed to share consistently and add value to my followers. You don't have to be a perfect writer or professorial at all. In fact, personal posts with images and unique metaphors and analogies for business and work engage more people. Just be you, and you will find your people.

- Seek mentorship. I mentioned this earlier in the book, but it's worth mentioning again, because this journey you are on needs outside help. Identify potential mentors within your organization or industry who can provide guidance and support. Building relationships with experienced professionals can accelerate your career development. For example, reach out to a senior professional whose career path you admire and ask if they would be willing to mentor you. Don't forget to stay in touch with your contacts through messages, meetings, or social media interactions. Networking is not just about making connections but also maintaining them.

While you are considering ways to build your professional network, you also need to be thinking about how you can stand out in the crowded market as an employee, entrepreneur, or community leader. Let's look at some strategies to help you build that brand that helps you show your stuff and make you voice shine.

Personal Branding

Your personal brand is how you present yourself to the world. It reflects your values, skills, and unique contributions. A strong personal brand can enhance your professional reputation and open up new opportunities. You don't need to be an author, a TikTok influencer, or a celebrity to build a brand.

I would have to say that I built a personal brand a bit based upon my circumstances, and then I became more intentional. When I experienced that layoff years back, it was painful, and at the same time the organizational leaders who had to deliver the message and help me exit the organization did so with compassion. I found LinkedIn as an outlet to share my views on employee and customer experience and even write articles on how to lay people off with dignity. While I didn't expect to be an entrepreneur at that time, my thoughts in my post attracted people to my work and the solutions I presented. People began reaching out, asking me to help their organization listen better to customers and employees. Their interest prompted me to start my own business.

While you might not be in the same position, think of who you are now and will become into the future as your brand, which means every decision you make is reflected in that too. Here are some ways to intentionally build a brand you can be proud of:

- First, identify your strengths, by reflecting on your skills, achievements, and what sets you apart from others. Understanding your strengths is the first step in building your personal brand. This might look like you are listing your top skills and accomplishments, such as specific projects you've led or unique expertise you possess.

- Second, define your brand message by crafting a clear and concise message that communicates your unique value proposition. This should highlight what you bring to the table and what you stand for. For example, if you are a project manager, create a personal brand statement like "I am a dedicated project manager with a passion for driving innovative solutions and fostering team collaboration." This can go on all your social channels and be a part of how you introduce yourself too.

- Third, create an online presence, by using social media platforms, a personal website, or a blog to showcase your expertise and share your insights. Regularly update your profiles with your latest achievements and projects. For example, you can start a blog where you share industry insights, project experiences, and professional tips. I know many people who did this well while also being in a full-time job.

- Fourth, seek opportunities for visibility by looking for chances to speak at conferences, write for industry publications, or participate in webinars. These activities help establish you as a thought leader in your field. This might look like you submitting a proposal to speak at an industry conference on a topic you're passionate about. This is not as hard as you might think. People are seeking free sources of reputable content everywhere. You just have to seek and you shall find.

- Finally, do a brand audit, by regularly seeking feedback from colleagues, mentors, and peers on your brand perception and how you can improve. This helps ensure your personal brand remains relevant and impactful. For example, ask a trusted colleague to review your LinkedIn profile and provide suggestions for improvement. I did this before, and it's really useful to hear from someone not so close to the source. The most important thing to focus on is ensuring that your personal brand is consistent across all platforms and interactions. Authenticity is key; your brand should genuinely reflect who you are and what you stand for. Get clear on this and your voice will be clear to anyone watching.

By actively participating in visible roles, building a robust professional network, and developing a strong personal brand, you can enhance your influence and advance your career. These strategies will help you assert your presence, share your unique contributions, and connect with others who can support your professional journey. While I don't like to harp on the negative, I do think that we need to remain pragmatic and understand the barriers and challenges that might pop up when using our voice to be seen.

Using Your Voice and Being Seen

In the journey of self-leadership, it's crucial to recognize and navigate both external and internal barriers that may silence your voice or hinder your visibility. This section will help you identify cultural and organizational barriers, as well as personal barriers, and provide strategies and tools to overcome them.

Overcoming Cultural and Organizational Barriers

Cultural and organizational barriers can create environments where certain voices are marginalized or ignored. These barriers can stem from entrenched hierarchies, lack of diversity, and implicit biases within the workplace. In rigid hierarchies, decision-making power is often concentrated at the top, making it difficult for lower-level employees to be heard. In a study conducted by my firm, Employee Fanatix, "48.6% of senior leadership claimed there were no barriers, significantly differing from 30.6% of mid-level and 30.1% of entry-level employees. This discrepancy underscores a tangible gap between senior leadership perceptions and the sentiments of entry and mid-level employees" (Employee Fanatix, LLC 2024). If you perceive this to be true in your organization, you aren't imagining it. It is very real.

Homogeneous work environments may overlook or undervalue diverse perspectives. Unconscious biases can affect who is listened to and whose ideas are given importance. In the study I referenced above, when asked to agree or disagree with the statement "I feel like my supervisor/boss actively listens to the things I say," 64% of women agreed, compared to 76% of men, showing a 12% gap in agreement level, which illustrates the different experiences at work based upon gender (Employee Fanatix, LLC 2024). Again, this is very real. Don't let it be daunting, but let it serve as the fuel for you to dive deeper into the ways to navigate or bypass the barriers.

Here are some useful strategies to navigate systemic barriers that might stand in your way on your journey to achieving more at work:

- Form alliances with colleagues who share your values and goals. A collective voice can be more powerful than a single one. For example, join or create employee resource groups (ERGs) that focus on diversity and inclusion to amplify your voice and the voices of others. If

  A collective voice can be more powerful than a single one.

  you are not part of one of the marginalized groups, there is also a growing trend for business resource groups (BRGs) where team members come together to conquer business issues in creative ways.

- Utilize formal channels for feedback and suggestions, such as town hall meetings, suggestion boxes, or diversity councils. These are places that you can use as venues to voice your ideas and concerns.

- Advocate for organizational changes that promote inclusivity and diverse voices. This might include pushing for bias training, inclusive hiring practices, and transparent decision-making processes. If your organization doesn't have it already, you could advocate for the implementation of a formal mentorship program aimed at supporting underrepresented employees.

Remember, self-leadership involves continuous growth and persistence, and each step you take toward using your voice and being seen contributes to your overall development and success. The positive impacts of being seen and heard at work, at home, and in your community are vast, which will lead you to experience pride in the journey you are uniquely on.

The Personal Impact of Being Seen and Heard

As I said in the beginning of this chapter, this is a full-circle moment. The benefits of using your voice and being seen extend beyond the workplace. These practices can also positively impact your personal life, leading to greater confidence, stronger relationships, and a more fulfilling life, which are elements of strong self-leadership.

In the very first chapter, we dove into self-worth and self-confidence, which really is an inside job. When you commit to demonstrating the courage to use your voice to be seen, you will see the ripple effects at the foundations of your living experience. Below are the some of the benefits to leaning into your unique voice and expressing it often:

When you commit to demonstrating the courage to use your voice to be seen, you will see the ripple effects at the foundations of your living experience.

- Boosting confidence: Regularly using your voice builds self-confidence, making you more comfortable in various social settings. Confidently expressing your opinions in social gatherings can lead to deeper, more meaningful conversations and connections.

- Building trust: Being open and communicative with friends and family builds trust and strengthens your relationships.

For example, sharing your thoughts and feelings honestly with loved ones fosters a deeper sense of understanding and connection.

- Achieving personal goals: The confidence and skills you develop by using your voice can help you achieve personal goals and pursue passions outside of work. This might look like starting a community project or pursuing a hobby you're passionate about, which can bring a sense of fulfillment and purpose.

Using your voice and being seen are powerful tools for personal and professional growth. These practices not only help you achieve greater visibility and career advancement, but also contribute to a more inclusive and innovative workplace culture. By embracing self-leadership and encouraging diverse voices, you can drive positive change both within yourself and in your organization.

Bright Ideas for Self-Leadership

Daily Reflection Journal: To enhance self-awareness and understand what your voice represents, use a notebook or digital platform to create a daily reflection journal. Each evening, spend 10–15 minutes reflecting on your day. Focus on moments when you spoke up or wished you had.

Prompt Questions:
- What did I speak up about today? How did it feel?
- Was there a moment I wanted to speak up but didn't? Why not?
- How did others respond to my input?

At the end of each week, review your entries to identify patterns and areas for improvement. This exercise will help you become more aware of how and when you use your voice, highlighting opportunities for growth and areas where you can be more assertive.

Voice Activation Challenge: This helps you to practice using your voice in various settings and to build confidence. Aim to speak up at least once in every meeting or group discussion you participate in for a week. Before each meeting, prepare one or two key points or questions you can contribute. Keep a log of each instance where you spoke up, noting the context, what you said, and the response you received. At the end of the week, reflect on your experiences. What felt challenging? What went well? How can you build on these experiences? Based on the feedback, develop a plan to address any areas for improvement. After a few weeks, follow up with the same individuals to assess your progress.

Conclusion: Are You Ready and Willing to Become a Strong Self-Leader?

We have become a world of waiters and blamers. We spend most of our time *waiting* for others to give us permission, grant us access, allot us a budget, invite us into their circle, give us time off, and tell us we are good enough, and then we *blame* them when they do not do these things. Sadly, many have given up the majority of their own power to determine what their life journey looks like to other people who will never act on their behalf to fulfill them in the ways they know they need. Many people are not willing to do the work that is required to discover and take back their own power and learn to lead themselves well despite their background and circumstances. I did not write this book for them.

> *We spend time* waiting *for others to give us permission, grant access, allot a budget, invite us into their circle, give us time off, and tell us we are good enough, and then we* blame *them when they do not do these things.*

I suppose my entire personal and professional journey has prepared me to write this book. I could not have written it in my 20s, because at that point I did not have the foresight to know all the ways that the hills and valleys would form me and make my experiences useful for others. From a childhood peppered with exclusion, addiction, and no silver spoon, to adult

217

experiences of layoffs, reorganizations, lost friends, and new alliances, I am, like all of you, a product of my past.

At times I have been the person who was waiting for green lights in a holding pattern that seemed to stop me from achieving all I wanted. I am not perfect. I am not imparting this message because I am leading myself well in *all* areas. I wrote this book because I have been there and done that, and I have some learnings that I'd like to share and some lessons I still have yet to learn. I would also love to hear from you so that you can share some of your learnings with me.

The one area of my life I am most proud of is not that I have not made mistakes, but that I have and that I recovered more quickly than most and immediately sought to learn from every one of them and to change my actions as a result. I occasionally whine about what might be happening to me, and then I remember that I am the only one who can lead me the way I deserve to be led. The same applies to you.

I occasionally whine about what might be happening to me, and then I remember that I am the only one who can lead me the way I deserve to be led.

At the beginning of this book, I shared with you my definition of self-leadership, which is the journey of growing inwardly to shine outwardly, spiraling upwards through self-awareness, resilience, and purposeful action. Another inspirational example that embodies this definition is Malala Yousafzai.

Malala's journey of self-leadership began with a strong sense of self-awareness. Growing up in the Swat Valley of Pakistan, she became acutely aware of the importance of education and the systemic barriers preventing girls from accessing it. Her awareness of these injustices and her own values around education and equality shaped her actions and advocacy from a young age (Malala Fund n.d.).

As a young girl, Malala was aware of the Taliban's growing influence and their ban on girls' education. Despite the dangers, she began blogging for the BBC under a pseudonym, writing about life under the Taliban and her desire for girls to have the right to go to school. This self-awareness and understanding of her values and the broader social context fueled her determination to speak out (Malala Fund n.d.).

Malala's resilience is remarkable. At the age of 15, she survived an assassination attempt by the Taliban, who targeted her for her outspoken advocacy for girls' education. Her ability to recover from such a traumatic event and continue her fight for education rights demonstrates extraordinary resilience (Malala Fund n.d.).

After being shot in the head by a Taliban gunman, Malala was flown to the UK for medical treatment. Despite the severity of her injuries, she made a remarkable recovery and continued to advocate for education. Her resilience shone through as she addressed the United Nations on her sixteenth birthday, stating, "They thought that the bullets would silence us, but they failed. And out of that silence came thousands of voices" (Malala Fund n.d.).

Malala's actions have always been purposeful, driven by her commitment to education and equality. She co-authored the memoir *I Am Malala*, and she established the Malala Fund to bring awareness to the social and economic impact of girls' education.

In 2014, at the age of 17, Malala was awarded the Nobel Peace Prize for her struggle against the suppression of children and young people and for the right of all children to receive an education. Through the Malala Fund, she continues to work toward ensuring that every girl has access to 12 years of free, safe, and quality education. Her purposeful actions have had a global impact, inspiring countless others to join the fight for education and equality (Malala Fund n.d.).

Malala Yousafzai's journey exemplifies the core principles of self-leadership. While our lives might not be as dramatic and earn us a Nobel Prize, there is much we can learn from her. Her self-awareness allowed her to understand the importance of education and her role in advocating for it. Her resilience enabled her to overcome a life-threatening attack and continue her mission with even greater determination. Her purposeful actions have led to significant advancements in global education rights and inspired millions. Malala's story is a powerful reminder that self-leadership involves growing inwardly to shine outwardly, using one's experiences and values to drive impactful change. By following her example, we can strive to lead ourselves and others with courage, resilience, and a deep sense of purpose.

We have developed a sort of codependence on our powerlessness. We hate that we do not have more control and influence over the journey we take in our lives, but then we will not do enough to take back that same control and influence. Then we sit in our own muck and pretend we do not have a hand in it.

I know that I gave you a lot to digest in this book. I created a short acronym that helps ground us in self-leadership in a memorable way – GROW.

Growth: Developing oneself from within

Resilience: Bouncing back and moving forward with grace

Outwardly: Extending one's influence and impact into the world

Wisdom: Leveraging insights and experiences for continuous improvement

I set out to help you grow, mostly by your own focus and attention to the principles I placed here, especially for you. This book is part self-help, part career development, and part leadership development. I mean to help you as a whole person, not just part of you. Imagine a life over which you have more control and influence, and when hopping out of the bed in the morning, you say, "Damn, I am powerful and competent and worthy and energized!" instead of "I wonder what xyz will make me focus on today and how far that will set me back from who I want to become." That would be a great day, wouldn't it? You can get there, I promise!

Where Do You Go from Here?

Like I always say, you have more power than you think. You can choose to use that power to lead yourself in a strong and self-directed way. You can choose to think and *be* different than you are today, allowing you to stretch and grow and make others want to be around you and follow you, not because of your title, but simply by how you show up. Just put one foot in front of the other. Do not think of the reasons why you cannot do these things, but think of exactly how you can.

How can you grow in self-leadership specifically? By doing the following:

- Understanding your intrinsic worth
- Understanding your limitations
- Understanding your fears
- Deciding between progress and perfection
- Prioritizing self-care
- Owning the three stages of empowerment
- Keying into your strengths
- Living relationship-building in action
- Leaning into flexible thinking
- Expecting clear expectations
- Realizing feedback is a gift
- Using your voice and being seen

While I have provided you with a plethora of ideas, tips, strategies, tools, and activities to help you grow in self-leadership, I would be operating counter to my belief that "it takes a village" to create real change if I did not provide other ways for you to hold yourself accountable to real change. Keep reading if you want to do more than simply reading this book and choosing to change nothing.

How Can You Remain Accountable?

Let me just say that I am a bit of an adaptation freak. I believe that with new insights, quantitative and qualitative, any person and any organization can choose to change. While we can make that change by listening to our gut, I find it longer lasting if we make the change because of more objective ways to measure our progress.

I deeply believe in the power of community to help each of its members grow and stretch and learn more than they can alone. To that extent, I have created an application for those interested in one of my Success Circles, which are made up of 12 people who are already on a strong path to self-leadership, but want accountability and community on the journey and they want access to me. Read the following section, "Success Circle," if you want to know more about this because you will need to DM me to get access to the application. You can also access a Self-Leadership Feedback Self-Assessment too. Also, remember to subscribe to my email list at heatheryounger .com, where I offer many free articles, videos, studies, and tools as well.

In the introduction to this book, I shared the story of the Golden Buddha, and how it was covered in clay, which hid its brilliance from all the world. For you reading this, your growth in self-leadership is the hammer and chisel with which you will gently remove the clay covering you to reveal your inner brilliance. Only you can determine how much clay you remove. Only you can choose whether or not to give away your power or lean into the power you possess to reveal your golden core.

No matter where you are on this journey, you can make different choices despite your circumstances. No more waiting, no more blaming, just a life full of self-love, inner peace, outward shine, deeply fulfilling relationships, and the ability to bounce back like you have never seen. If more people commit to this type of change, we will become a world that embraces our own responsibility to show up differently, with strength, empathy, self-compassion, and an undeniable inner glow. We can create a canvas filled with light and color and a unique blend of self-discovery and empowerment. I have given you the palette and the tools to help us get here. It is up to each of you to pick them up and use them for your own benefit and for those who look to you for guidance and leadership in some way.

Success Circle

You are a competent leader who manages at least one person and you are on the right path with culture. But you want to catch Culture Slip™ before it silently creeps in, resulting in turnover you do not see coming and missed goals and opportunities.

Any leader can create magnetic cultures by using the Caring Leadership® process because it teaches you exactly how to show your people you care by changing leader behaviors.

Whether your team consists of you and one other person or hundreds of people, Caring Leadership is the *only* process that creates magnetic cultures through our proprietary Nine-Step Behavior Change Model.

Stop allowing Culture Slip. Transform into a Caring Leader which starts with Self-Leadership.

What's Different

Old leadership training models involved passive listening on the part of trainees and a heavy focus on theory.

The new Caring Leadership process is rooted in active listening and tangible, results-oriented behavior change.

Learn more about Caring Leadership and inquire about my success circles meant to grow the leader within you at https://www.caringleadershiplearning.com/success-circle.

Free Self-Assessment on Feedback Styles and Opportunities for Growth

What is your feedback style? Understanding your feedback style and identifying opportunities for growth in this area can significantly enhance your self-leadership skills.

Take the free self-assessment to evaluate your current approach to giving and receiving feedback and pinpoint areas for improvement. Get yours free at https://www.caringleadership learning.com/feedback-assessment

DiSC® Assessment with 20-Minute Review

DiSC® is a widely used personal assessment tool, helping over a million individuals each year enhance teamwork, communication, and productivity in the workplace. Organizations and facilitators leverage these profiles to drive cultural transformation, fostering lasting behavioral changes that positively impact their workforce. Individuals leverage their profiles as part of their personal and professional development process to help reach their full potential.

Here's how it works:

1. **Take the assessment**. Spend 15–20 minutes answering around 80 questions in the adaptive DiSC model test to determine your fit within the four main personality reference styles.

2. **Receive your profile**. Upon completion, you'll receive a personalized profile detailing your unique behavioral style, strategies for engaging with others, your needs, and preferred environment.

3. **Personal review**. Enjoy a 20-minute review session with Heather R. Younger to further understand your results and how to apply them effectively.

Embark on this journey to gain deeper insights into yourself and others.

Get started at: https://www.caringleadershiplearning.com/DISC.

References

Ackerman, C. E., & Nash, J. (2018, November 6). "What Is Self-Worth & How Do We Build it? (Incl. Worksheets)." *Positive Psychology*. Retrieved April 26, 2024, from https://positivepsychology.com/self-worth/

Bar-Haim, Y., Lamy, D., Pergamin-Hight, L., Bakermans-Kranenburg, M., & van IJzendoorn. (2007). "Threat -related Attentional Bias in Anxious and Non-anxious Individuals: A Meta Analytic Study." *Psychological Bulletin* 133, 1–24.

Cleveland Clinic. "5 Signs That You Might Be a Perfectionist — and How to Find Balance." (2023, May 4). Cleveland Clinic Health Essentials. Retrieved April 29, 2024, from https://health.clevelandclinic.org/signs-of-perfectionism

Cohan, P. (2024, March 6). "Why Innovation Matters: Lessons from the iPhone." *Inc.* magazine. Retrieved July 2, 2024, from https://www.inc.com/peter-cohan/why-innovation-matters-lessons-from-iphone.html

Comaford, C. (2019, July 3). "76% of People Think Mentors Are Important, But Only 37% Have One." *Forbes*. Retrieved July 2, 2024, from https://www.forbes.com/sites/christinecomaford/2019/07/03/new-study-76-of-people-think-mentors-are-important-but-only-37-have-one/

Danao, M. (2024, April 30). "How to Perform a Job Analysis (2024 Guide)." *Forbes*. Retrieved July 4, 2024, from https://www.forbes.com/advisor/business/job-analysis/

Dweck, C. S. (2006). *Mindset: The New Psychology of Success*. Random House Publishing Group.

Employee Fanatix, LLC. (2024, April 1). "Adapting to Hybrid Realities: A Study on Workplace Culture and the Crucial Element of Listening in 2024." Retrieved July 6, 2024, from https://drive.google.com/file/d/18khOTgui75W1bPJuG6FYtmPTlb3az40L/view

Hall, K. (2014, July 12). "Self-Validation." *Psychology Today*. Retrieved April 25, 2024, from https://www.psychologytoday.com/us/blog/pieces-mind/201407/self-validation

Hoffman, R., Casnocha, B., & Yeh, C. (2014). *The Alliance: Managing Talent in the Networked Age*. Harvard Business Review Press.

Hughes, M. (2017, November 9). "I am a Fraud; I Think You're a Fraud, Too." YouTube.com. Retrieved April 25, 2024, from https://youtu.be/bHkf7-b3jVE?si=MqQD2lXwSXXVOoHH

Javanbakht, A., & Saab, L. (2017, October 27). "What Happens in the Brain When We Feel Fear." *Smithsonian*. Retrieved April 29, 2024, from https://www.smithsonianmag.com/science-nature/what-happens-brain-feel-fear-180966992/

MacLeod, C., & Mathews, A. (2012). "Cognitive Bias Modification Approaches to Anxiety." *Annual Review of Clinical Psychology* 8, 189–217. https://doi.org/10.1146/annurev-clinpsy-032511-143052

Malala Fund. (n.d.). "Malala's Story." Retrieved July 6, 2024, from https://malala.org/malalas-story

Martin, S. (2023, September 8). "8 Simple Ways to Increase Self-Compassion." *Psychology Today*. Retrieved June 12, 2024, from https://www.psychologytoday.com/us/blog/conquering-codependency/202306/8-simple-strategies-to-boost-self-compassion

Miller, L. (2021, June 15). "What Is Cognitive Flexibility, and Why Does It Matter?" BetterUp. Retrieved July 3, 2024, from https://www.betterup.com/blog/cognitive-flexibility

Mind Tools Content Team. "Achieving Personal Empowerment: Taking Charge of Your Life and Career." (n.d.). Mind Tools. Retrieved June 10, 2024, from https://www.mindtools.com/aiaydss/achieving-personal-empowerment

NASA Safety Center. (2009, April 1). "Lost in Translation." NASA.gov. Retrieved July 4, 2024, from https://sma.nasa.gov/docs/default-source/safety-messages/safetymessage-2009-08-01-themarsclimateorbitermishap.pdf?sfvrsn=eaa1ef8_4

Nelson Mandela Foundation. (n.d.). "Biography of Nelson Mandela – Nelson Mandela Foundation." Nelson Mandela Foundation. Retrieved July 6, 2024, from https://www.nelsonmandela.org/biography

Neuhaus, M. (2020, November 17). "What Is Self-Leadership? Models, Theory, and Examples." *PositivePsychology*. https://positivepsychology.com/self-leadership/#:~:text=Self%2DLeadership%20Explained,-Self%2Dleadership%20is&text=Manz%20(1983)%2C%20who%20later,%E2%80%9D%20(Manz%2C%201986).

Psychology Today. (n.d.). "Imposter Syndrome." Retrieved June 26, 2024, from https://www.psychologytoday.com/us/basics/imposter-syndrome

Quast, L. (2011, October 31). "How Becoming a Mentor Can Boost Your Career." *Forbes.* Retrieved July 2, 2024, from https://www.forbes.com/sites/lisaquast/2011/10/31/how-becoming-a-mentor-can-boost-your-career/

"Self-Awareness Theory." (2024, April 15). Encyclopedia.com. Retrieved April 25, 2024, from https://www.encyclopedia.com/social-sciences/applied-and-social-sciences-magazines/self-awareness-theory

Southern, M. G. (2023, October 24). "Majority of Social Media Users Admit They'd Be Happier If It Didn't Exist." *Search Engine Journal.* Retrieved April 25, 2024, from https://www.searchenginejournal.com/majority-of-social-media-users-admit-theyd-be-happier-if-it-didnt-exist/499193/

Stevens, L., & Kemp, A. (2023, September 27). "How to Strengthen and Sustain Workplace Culture Using Recognition." Gallup. Retrieved June 27, 2024, from https://www.gallup.com/workplace/511592/strengthen-sustain-workplace-culture-using-recognition.aspx

World Health Organization (WHO). (n.d.). *Self-Care for Health and Well-Being.* Retrieved June 7, 2024, from https://www.who.int/health-topics/self-care#tab=tab_1

Younger, H. R. (2023a, October 11). "Communicating with Clarity as a Manager." LinkedIn Learning. Retrieved July 1, 2024, from https://www.linkedin.com/learning/communicating-with-clarity-as-a-manager/shifting-from-vague-to-clear-communications

Younger, H. R. (2023b, November 9). "Active Listening for Better Leadership Communication." LinkedIn Learning. Retrieved July 1, 2024, from https://www.linkedin.com/learning/active-listening-for-better-leadership-communication/active-listening-the-key-leadership-skill

Younger, H. R., & Curtain, J. (2024, June 17). "How to Create Positive Work Environments - An Interview with Jennifer Curtin." *Leadership With Heart* podcast. Retrieved July 2, 2024, from https://podcasts.apple.com/us/podcast/how-to-create-positive-work-environments-an/id1366572251?i=1000659356031

Zak, P. J. (2017, January–February). "The Neuroscience of Trust." *Harvard Business Review.* https://hbr.org/2017/01/the-neuroscience-of-trust

Acknowledgments

To the Wiley team: Cheryl Segura, thank you for your support. I appreciate your candid advice and listening to my ideas. It means a lot. Amanda Pyne, thank you for your assistance on the creative book covers and your guidance. Tom Dinse, thank you for helping me develop my ideas and bring this book to life. Sangeetha Suresh, thank you for your contributions to making this book the best it could be.

To the Employee Fanatix team: Ashley Rivera, thank you for always knowing the words that I would say and keeping me honest through this book-writing process. Your help and support mean more than you know. Hathaway Rabette, thank you for holding down the fort with the business when I needed to take deep dives to focus on finishing this book and for always having my back. Jen DeVore, thank you for being the only person who moves more quickly than I do to help me shine and make the work I do reveal itself in creative ways. Neil Hughes, you have been with me on my podcast journey since 2018, but we have been friends many more years before that. Thank you for giving me honest feedback and allowing me to continue my podcast, which allowed me to insert some of the episode snippets in this book. Cristy O'Connor, thank you for serving as my business coach and believing in my ability to do hard things to build a better business and lead myself better, but not alone.

To my CMI Speaker Management team: Thank you for helping me elevate my game and grow into the leader I am today. Without your support and help, I could never have gotten to where I am today.

To my family: Luis, Gabriela, Sebastian, Dominic, and Matteo, thank you for supporting me even when I seemed flustered and frustrated over the process of writing this book. Thank you for giving me the space to write the words that will help others, and inspiring me to be better. Mom, you have always been a huge example of someone who leads themselves well. Even in your lowest time, you rose to become a strong role model for me and make great decisions that served you well.

To others who have helped me on this journey: To my closest friends, Kimberly Davis, Sarah Elkins, Sara Ross, Melissa Hughes, Sylvie Di Giusto, and Ghislaine Bruner, thank you for showing me the error in my thinking and in my ways and made it easier to course-correct to grow in self-leadership. To Barb, thank you for helping me get my health together so I could write this book from a place of integrity.

About the Author

Heather R. Younger, JD, CSP, is a trusted contributor to leading news outlets like Forbes, Fast Company, Bloomberg, NBC, and ABC and one of the world's leading experts on Caring Leadership® and active listening at work. She is the visionary founder and CEO of Employee Fanatix, a preeminent employee engagement and workplace culture consulting firm to Fortune 100 companies. Employee Fanatix conducts annual research on workplace culture, relying on employee voices for what is relevant now, to help companies redefine their culture strategy. Heather has personally read over 30,000 employee surveys and facilitated over 100 employee focus groups, including her signature "Art of Active Listening Sessions."

With over 25 years of successfully managing teams, she has worked in customer experience, sales, and large account management for multimillion-dollar accounts and multiple industries such as tech, staffing, healthcare, professional services, the public sector, and the financial sector. She's a renowned keynote speaker, drawing insights from current data and putting into practice what she teaches in her Caring Leadership Transformation Model™.

Heather is an award-winning leader in the area of employee engagement as recognized by Inspiring Workplaces, is a LinkedIn Learning course partner, three-time best-selling author, TEDX speaker, and the host of the popular podcast *Leadership With Heart*.

Index

Note: Page references with *f* refer to figures.